Paw Prints in Heaven?

Paw Prints in Heaven?

Christians and Pet Loss

James L. McClinton PhD

iUniverse, Inc.
New York Lincoln Shanghai

Paw Prints in Heaven?
Christians and Pet Loss

iUniverse, Inc.

For information address:
iUniverse, Inc.
2021 Pine Lake Road, Suite 100
Lincoln, NE 68512
www.iuniverse.com

ISBN: 0-595-32228-X

Printed in the United States of America

In Memory Of
Teddy "Pooh" Bear
February 18, 1991–September 14, 2003

Dedication

This book is respectfully dedicated to you, the reader. You would not be reading this now if you didn't love animals and were not somehow concerned about the loss of a beloved pet. It is my sincere hope that this book will help you find the comfort you seek in God's word. Until the day you see your companion once again, I pray that God will grant you the peace of knowing that the "Judge of all the earth" will "do right."

CONTENTS

INTRODUCTION

Why I wrote this book

Over the years, I've watched Christian parents struggle as they tried to explain the status of a deceased pet to their children. I've also seen a number of adults deeply troubled by the loss of a pet, not knowing what God's will for those animals really is. Those who have suffered the loss of a beloved pet will agree that no words can adequately convey the grief and overwhelming sorrow that is experienced during one of life's most traumatic events. Such a loss can be especially difficult for Christians as they struggle to reconcile their thoughts, beliefs, and actions with Biblical doctrine and church teachings.

Try to imagine the peace that troubled souls would enjoy after losing a cherished pet if they knew with certainty that they would see their little companions again in eternity. And wouldn't it be wonderful if a Christian parent could look his or her child straight in the eye and promise them with conviction that they will see their "best friend" again in heaven? Good News! That is exactly what *The Bible* tells us!

God blessed our family with a precious little pet. We loved him deeply and his love for us was no less profound. When he passed away, my wife and I did the best we could to console each other as we struggled to bear the heavy burden of grief and sadness. *The Bible* was a tremendous source of comfort and reassurance as the days slowly passed, but comfort in dealing with our grief was not the only thing we looked for in God's word. Suddenly we found ourselves wondering if God would allow a love such as ours to simply die and fade into oblivion. We wanted to know what *The Bible* had to say about animals in eternity.

Considering the number of other Christians who have surely wanted to know God's design for animals in eternity, I couldn't understand why I had never heard the subject preached or discussed in a Christian context. I was also puzzled as to why I had never seen anything written on

1

the subject. Hungry for answers, I set out for the nearest Christian book-store to see what I could find. Much to my surprise, I found nothing there or anywhere else. It was then that I realized that I would have to search God's word for answers to my questions about His plan for animals, and I vowed to share them with other believers. Part One of this book guides the reader through a systematic study of God's word with respect to the question of animals and eternity. Each finding of fact is justified with scriptural references and the final conclusion is reinforced with a graphic representation.

All pet owners will eventually have to deal with the loss of their little companions. Unfortunately, many of us wait until our pets are terminally ill or have passed away before facing the difficult decisions that must be made. Because it's so painful, many pet owners choose not to think about losing their pets and put it off until it's too late. Then, when the time of sorrow comes upon them and their world is turned upside down, they find themselves struggling to cope with their loss while having to make the necessary final arrangements.

Difficult decisions such as when to stop expensive medical treatments that aren't working, or whether or not euthanasia is the best course of action, are hard enough before becoming burdened with the loss of a pet. But, dealing with these and other pet death related issues while in the midst of grief can seem impossible. I wrote Part Two of this book to help Christians come to terms with the difficult issues associated with pet loss. Though every loss is unique, they all share common traits that every pet owner should be aware of. Many necessary decisions and arrangements can, and should, be addressed now, before the loss occurs. Thinking about the "unthinkable" ahead of time will help you take certain steps that will eliminate a lot of unnecessary stress and anxiety later.

The truths I discovered while writing this book were a tremendous comfort to us as we dealt with our loss and I pray that they will be a blessing to you in your time of grief as well. Rejoice, because now you can know with certainty that all will be well with your little companions in eternity. We must mourn our losses, but only for a season. Let's spend the rest of our lives celebrating the victory that we'll enjoy when we see our friends again in the presence of God.

I know your pain

My wife and I acquired a Lhasa Apso puppy shortly after Hurricane Hugo devastated coastal South Carolina in 1989. Since the little guy's face looked just like a Teddy Bear's, we knew that "Teddy" was the perfect choice for a name.

Teddy was especially affectionate as a puppy and we both loved to hug him, just as a child hugs a real teddy bear. He was always in the midst of everything and his presence was a tremendous comfort to us as we went about rebuilding our hurricane-shattered lives. The unconditional love he gave us and the anxiety he suffered whenever we left him even for brief periods only endeared him to us that much more. It wasn't long before we considered Teddy a full-fledged member of our family.

Any doubts I ever had about whether or not animals had feelings vanished one day when I tried to take him outside. He was in a playful mood and no matter how hard I tried, I just couldn't grab him as he darted around my legs. In my frustration, I sat on the stairs, covered my face with both hands and pretended to cry. Only a few seconds had passed before I felt him licking the backs of my hands, his way of comforting me and assuring me that everything would be all right. I was careful not to let him know I'd tricked him. I returned his affection and waited a little while longer before I took him outside. Teddy showed his capacity to "feel" on many other occasions as well. But the incident I'll never forget occurred soon after I lost my oldest son to cancer. Teddy sensed my suffering and intentionally comforted me in his own special and unmistakable way.

As Teddy aged over the years, we became increasingly aware that he was changing. My wife and I occasionally discussed what life would be like without him. But, as you might imagine, those discussions were unpleasant and we always ended them as quickly as possible. We had read a lot about the breed and knew what Teddy's expected life span was, but our hearts overruled our minds and we simply chose to ignore the inevitable.

When Teddy was 9 years old, we were stunned to learn that he had developed cancer in his bladder and front leg. We knew surgery was his only hope for survival, but understood there were no guarantees it would succeed. Fearing the worst and hoping for the best, we decided to move as quickly as possible. In what was nothing less than a miracle, the surgery and therapy proved successful. But the joy we experienced after Teddy's deliverance from the ravages of his disease was tempered by the realization that we could no longer take his presence for granted. For the first time, we truly realized he would not be with us for the rest of our lives.

About three and a half years after his surgery, Teddy suddenly became very ill.We rushed him to emergency care, but soon learned our efforts were in vain. The cancer had returned in full force. We did not enjoy a sense of cautious optimism like we had after his successful surgery, because we somehow knew this situation was different. The cancer was in his pancreas and there was nothing anyone could do for him. Teddy's condition worsened rapidly and it was all too apparent that his pain was excruciating. Finally, his heartbreaking cries and yelps convinced us we had to bring an end to his terrible suffering. Less than 24 hours after we took him to the hospital, our little companion was gone.

Caveat emptor, let the buyer beware

As you are about to see, God's word gives us all the information we need in order to discern His will for animals. But, it's not a matter of simply picking up *The Bible* and turning to a single verse. We must seek God's truth by carefully studying His word while praying for knowledge. Only then will God enlighten us with the knowledge of His overall plan for creation. God's word assures us of this truth:

> Yea, if thou criest after knowledge, and liftest up thy voice for understanding; If thou seekest her as silver, and searchest for her as for hid treasures; Then shalt thou understand the fear of the Lord, and find the knowledge of God. Proverbs 2:3-5 (KJV)

Writing this book was a labor of love. Though I had read *The Bible* from cover to cover seven times, God's word appeared as fresh and relevant to me during my search for answers as it did the first time I read it. In seeking God's plan for animals in eternity, I prayed for understanding, sought the opinions of other Christians, most notably my wife, and made a thorough study of God's word. God rewarded those efforts by revealing His remarkable truth to me, and I'm pleased to share my newfound knowledge with all Christian pet owners.

Whether or not you agree with my findings and conclusions has no bearing on your salvation. Embracing my beliefs will not get you to heaven, and shunning them will not send you to hell. Even so, I encourage you to undertake your own search for God's truth. Remember, *The Bible* warns us that we are to exercise caution when embracing the beliefs of others and to put those beliefs to the test:

> *Beloved, believe not every spirit, but try the spirits whether they are of God…1 John 4:1 (KJV)*

I strongly suggest you base your own beliefs about animals and eternity on God's word. And, when discussing those beliefs with others, you should be prepared to justify them with specific references to scripture. People can be quick to defend a belief by saying, *"The Bible* says so!" But, more often than not, their arguments fail when they're asked for specific scriptural references.

Finally, you must be especially careful when discussing the eternal destiny of animals with children. If you promise a child that his or her pet will go to "doggie heaven" without giving them Bible-based justification, the child may be unable to distinguish your explanation from stories about the Tooth Fairy, Easter Bunny, Santa Claus, and other childhood fairy tales. If the child is too young to understand scripture, at least let him or her know that God's word is the source of your beliefs and that they will understand when they're a little older.

P🐾w Prints
in Heaven?

PART ONE

CHAPTER ONE

PETS AND ETERNITY

What *The Bible does not* say

Imagine how nice it would be to pick up *The Bible*, turn to a section where the words are printed in red ink, and read something like this: "Thou may taketh comfort in knowing that the Lord thy God has reserved a place for your beloved pet in his heavenly realm." Yes, it would be wonderful indeed. But, as many Christians already know, you will not find anything like that in a single verse or passage of holy scripture.

Does God condemn people who have to steal in order to eat, or those who kill other human beings in war? Is salvation given to infants who die at an early age, or people who go insane? Does *The Bible* say anything about violating speeding laws or running STOP signs? Does it contain a single verse that tells us what to do when we discover a grocery store cashier has made a mistake and given us too much change? The absence of specific references to these and other issues does not mean we should simply ignore them.

Contrary to what many would have you believe, *The Bible does* address animal-related issues such as death and eternity, but not in a direct way. This is likely because animals are not the focus of God's word, a distinction that belongs exclusively to man. When *The Bible* appears to be silent on a particular issue, we must seek God's truth by undertaking a systematic study of the word while praying that God will bless us with understanding. Only then will God reveal his incredible truths to us. Such is the case with the question of animals in eternity.

When Christians lose a beloved pet, many feel confused and are unsure about what happens to them after death. Ignorance of God's word can make them vulnerable, and many reach out in desperation to embrace false beliefs. Many want to believe their beloved pets will go to heaven, but have no idea what *The Bible* says. Some search God's word for obvious answers, then become discouraged when they don't find them. Others simply listen to their hearts or jump to false conclusions without taking the time to see what *The Bible* says. As Christians, we must not allow sorrow and grief to distort God's truth and deceive us into embracing false beliefs and practices. God specifically condemns such behavior in *The Bible*.

There are many obstacles impeding any study of God's word. For example, it's our human nature to take words and concepts out of context. We also like to embellish the "letter" of scripture in order to "clarify" God's truth. While subtle changes may seem inconsequential, their end product can be something contrary to the "spirit" (or intent) of God's intended message. Finally, two thousand years of church tradition has been blended with a number of secular beliefs to displace many Biblical truths. There are many examples, but let's look at just a few of the more common ones:

- *The Bible* does not refer to "three" wise men visiting the infant Jesus the night of his birth or mention any of their names;
- Jesus was not born on December 25 (this date comes from the pagan celebration of Saturnalia which occurred at the winter solstice);
- *The Bible* does not mention an apple in its account of man's fall in the Garden of Eden;
- Bunny rabbits, eggs and maypoles are all associated with pagan fertility rites and rituals and have nothing to do with the Messiah being crucified on the cross.

The Bible is not an itemized list of "do's and don'ts'," but a revelation of God's will for all of creation. It is a remarkable book in that God used an unusual combination of authors and languages in such a way that scripture will remain relevant to every culture in every age. Because some issues are absolute, God addressed them head-on (e.g. "thou shalt not kill"). But others are more complex and subject to many variables. In such cases, we have to follow a progression of truths found in different scriptures. A good example is eschatology, or the study of the "end times." References to the second coming of Christ, the rapture and tribulation period are scattered throughout the Old and New Testaments and all end time doctrines are based on various combinations and interpretations of those scriptures.

Animals are important to God, and He wants them to be important to us as well. After all, it wouldn't be consistent with God's plan for creation to overlook them or let them fade into oblivion after death. That's why *The Bible* tells us everything we need to know about them. God's word reveals that He did not create animals to rule over us, or to be considered our equals. God gave man "dominion" over the animals, but His word says it was His intention that they be a blessing to us. *The Bible* explains this relationship, as well other animal-related issues God wants us to understand. Jesus made it clear that God wants us to study the word as diligently as possible in order to discern His truths:

> *And I say unto you, Ask, and it shall be given you; seek, and ye shall find; knock, and it shall be opened unto you. For every one that asketh receiveth; and he that seeketh findeth; and to him that knock-eth it shall be opened. Luke 11:9-10 (KJV)*

> *And beside this, giving all diligence, add to your faith virtue; and to virtue knowledge. 2 Peter 1:5 (KJV)*

When God created man, He instilled within him the ability to love. He gave us this gift so that we might freely choose to enter into a loving relationship with Him. *The Bible* tells us that God also wants us to love one another and the rest of creation as well. But, not all love is the same. We cannot love another person the same way we love God. And, we cannot love an animal the same way we love another human being. But, as you will see, love is the key to understanding God's plan for creation, including the animals.

What *The Bible does* say

There are many aspects of our everyday lives we are unable to understand. For example, we still cannot explain or understand something as familiar as gravity, in spite of the fact that we live in an age of incredible technological advancements. Though God's word is clear, many of us can not grasp His plan for the salvation of man and don't understand why Jesus had to die on the cross. So how could we possibly expect to understand every aspect of His will for animals? As we're about to see, *The Bible* tells us that man was created in God's image. But that does not mean our knowledge and understanding is comparable to God's. Our insatiable curiosity drives us to seek answers to our questions about God, but there are many things we could never understand:

> *O the depth of the riches both of the wisdom and knowledge of God! How unsearchable are his judgments, and his ways past finding out! Romans 11:33 (KJV)*

Fortunately, God's plan for animals, with respect to eternal life, is *not* one of the mysteries God intends to keep hidden from man's understanding. As you are about to discover, God explains His plan of eternal life for all of creation in a clear and unmistakable way.

Before we commence our study, we must first acknowledge a key fundamental truth: Animals have never "fallen from grace" as mankind did in the Garden of Eden. Since animals do not have the ability to choose between good and evil, they cannot be considered "sinners." And, because they are sinless creatures, God does not condemn them to an eternity in hell. Remember, any animal conduct we consider "bad" is probably nothing more than a conflict between their God-given nature and our human expectations. Sadly, "undesirable" behavior may also be the result of abuse at the hand of man.

The Bible tells us that hell was created for "the devils and all his angels" after they rebelled against God. And when man exercised his free will and chose to do likewise, God sentenced him to the same punishment:

> *Then shall he say also unto them on the left hand, Depart from me, ye cursed, into everlasting fire, prepared for the devil and his angels: Matthew 25:41 (KJV)*

God created the animals for a reason and subsequently made them subject to man's authority. God also blessed man with the capacity for loving those animals, and I believe He gave animals the ability to return that love. While most Christians will agree it does not seem consistent with God's nature to allow mutual love to simply cease to exist when either creature dies, we must reconcile such a belief with the letter and spirit of His word.

In his compassionate wisdom, God has given us reason for hope and the assurance that we need not worry about seeing our pets in heaven. Does this mean that we should expect to see cockroaches, venomous snakes, and mosquitoes in heaven as well? As tragic as it may seem,

God's word warns us that many humans will not make it to heaven. It must, therefore, follow that many animals will not make it either.

As you discover how God's word tells us that some animals will spend eternity in His presence, you will want to know which ones will enjoy the privilege and how the selections will be made. By joining me in this pursuit of God's truth, I believe you are about to be blessed in ways you never imagined. Please walk with me in a step-by-step journey through scripture and let's see what God has revealed to us about animals and their eternal destiny.

A near miss?

There are many scriptures that speak of animals in, or descending from, heaven. But it is my considered opinion that God created (or will create) those creatures for the purpose of filling specific, pre-ordained roles. I don't believe those references can be offered as proof that animals will make the transition from mortality to immortality. Let's look at a few examples:

And I saw, and behold a white horse: and he that sat on him had a bow; and a crown was given unto him: and he went forth conquering, and to conquer. Revelation 6:2 (KJV)

And every creature which is in heaven, and on the earth, and under the earth, and such as are in the sea, and all that are in them, heard I saying, Blessing, and honour, and glory, and power, be unto him that sitteth upon the throne, and unto the Lamb for ever and ever. Revelation 5:13 (KJV)

And Elisha prayed, and said, Lord, I pray thee, open his eyes, that he may see. And the Lord opened the eyes of the young man; and he saw: and, behold, the mountain was full of horses and chariots of fire round about Elisha. 2 Kings 6:17 (KJV)

For the purpose of this study, we'll set these and other similar examples aside so we can see how God's word addresses common, earthbound animals.

CHAPTER TWO

ECCE HOMO! (BEHOLD THE MAN!)

Moving ahead to the distant past

The Bible tells us that in the beginning, God gave both man and animal unique and distinctive natures:

> *And God said, Let the waters bring forth abundantly the moving creature that hath life, and fowl that may fly above the earth in the open firmament of heaven. And God created great whales, and every living creature that moveth, which the waters brought forth abundantly, after their kind, and every winged fowl after his kind: and God saw that it was good. And God blessed them, saying, Be fruitful, and multiply, and fill the waters in the seas, and let fowl multiply in the earth. And the evening and the morning were the fifth day. And God said, Let the earth bring forth the living creature after his kind, cattle, and creeping thing, and beast of the earth after his kind: and it was so. And God made the beast of the earth after his kind, and cattle after their kind, and every thing that creepeth upon the earth after his kind: and God saw that it was good. And God said, Let us make man in our image, after our likeness: and let them have dominion over the fish of the sea, and over the fowl of the air, and over the cattle, and over all the earth, and over every creeping thing that creepeth upon the earth. Genesis 1:20-26 (KJV)*

In his letter to the Jewish Church (Hebrews), Paul affirms the fact that God created man different from the animals. Paul even goes so far as to cite our ranking in God's created order:

> *Thou madest him a little lower than the angels; thou crownedst him with glory and honour, and didst set him over the works of thy*

14

hands: Thou hast put all things in subjection under his feet. For in that he put all in subjection under him, he left nothing that is not put under him. But now we see not yet all things put under him. Hebrews 2:7-8 (KJV)

Let's take a look under the hood

In order to understand God's plan for animals, we must first understand His plan for man. The most significant difference between man and animal is the fact that man has the distinct privilege of being created in the "image" (or "likeness") of God:

*So God created man in his own **image**, in the image of God created he him; male and female created he them. Genesis 1:27 (KJV)*

*This is the book of the generations of Adam. In the day that God created man, in the **likeness** of God made he him; Genesis 5:1 (KJV)*

*Whoso sheddeth man's blood, by man shall his blood be shed: for in the **image** of God made he man. Genesis 9:6 (KJV)*

*And have put on the new man, which is renewed in knowledge after the **image** of him that created him: Colossians 3:10 (KJV)*

But what does "image" or "likeness" mean? Is this an enigma meant to be beyond man's understanding? When Michelangelo painted God on the ceiling of the Sistine Chapel, he depicted him as an old man with a long gray beard. While some of us will eventually resemble such an image in our old age, most women would not welcome such an interpretation. Many Christians feel this is another one of God's "mysteries" and that the explanation is simply beyond man's understanding. It is true that Jesus told us we can never fully understand God's mysteries and some things are simply beyond our understanding:

And he said, Unto you it is given to know the mysteries of the kingdom of God: but to others in parables; that seeing they might not see, and hearing they might not understand. Luke 8:10 (KJV)

Fortunately, the meaning of the words "image of God" is not one of the mysteries God never intended to reveal to us as some would choose to believe. God is faithful, and by His grace, He has blessed us with the ability to discern those things He wants us to understand:

Whereby, when ye read, ye may understand my knowledge in the mystery of Christ. Ephesians 3:4 (KJV)

But the natural man receiveth not the things of the Spirit of God: for they are foolishness unto him: neither can he know them, because they are spiritually discerned. 1 Corinthians 2:14 (KJV)

God's word tells us that God is a triune being existing in the form of the Father, Son, and Holy Ghost. His word also tells us that man is tri-une in nature as well, existing in the form of body, soul, and spirit. Simply said, this explains how we are created in His "image" (or "like-ness"). The essence of God is triune, and so it is with man as well.

THE TRIUNE NATURE OF GOD AND MAN

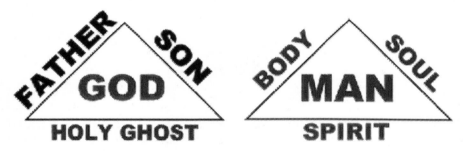

Many Christians are not aware of this Biblical truth and would argue that soul and spirit are the same thing. Let's see what God's word tells us. To begin with, *The Bible* makes numerous references to our mortal **bodies**, the **first part** of our triune nature. Here are just a couple of examples:

All go unto one place; all are of the dust, and all turn to dust again. Ecclesiastes 3:20 (KJV)

It is sown a natural body; it is raised a spiritual body. There is a nat-ural body, and there is a spiritual body. 1 Corinthians 15:44 (KJV)

God's Word tells us that the **second aspect** of man's essence is the **soul**. The writer of Genesis shows us that body and soul are distinct and separate aspects of our being:

> *And the Lord God formed man of the dust of the ground, and breathed into his nostrils the breath of life; and man became a living soul. Genesis 2:7 (KJV)*

Unlike the body, the soul does not necessarily perish at death. The Psalmist makes this truth abundantly clear:

> *But God will redeem my Soul from the power of the grave: for he shall receive me. Psalms 49:15 (KJV)*

> *For thou hast delivered my Soul from death, mine eyes from tears, and my feet from falling. Psalms 116:8 (KJV)*

Elijah also gave us a remarkable example of this truth:

> *And he stretched himself upon the child three times, and cried unto the Lord, and said, O Lord my God, I pray thee, let this child's Soul come into him again. And the Lord heard the voice of Elijah; and the soul of the child came into him again, and he revived. 1 Kings 17:21-22 (KJV)*

Our bodies are meant to be temporary "homes" only and they will eventually return to the dust from which they were made. So the soul is the dwelling place of our emotions and it is where our own self-awareness resides. It is the soul that accommodates the love (or hate) of God's creation.

The **third element** of man's triune nature is the **spirit**. In the following scriptures, Paul refers to the spirit in his letter to the Hebrews, and goes so far as to distinguish it from the soul:

> *For the word of God is quick, and powerful, and sharper than any two edged sword, piercing even to the dividing asunder of **soul** and **spirit**, and of the joints and marrow, and is a discerner of the thoughts and intents of the heart. Hebrews 4:12 (KJV)*

> *For as the **body** without the **spirit** is dead, so faith without works is dead also. James 2:26 (KJV)*

The spirit is the most significant part of our makeup and that which distinguishes us from the rest of God's creation. Jesus told us that without the spirit, we cannot worship God:

> *God is a **spirit**: and they that worship him must worship him in **spirit** and in truth. John 4:24 (KJV)*

Paul affirms Jesus' words in his letter to the church at Corinth:

> *Now we have received, not the spirit of the world, but the **spirit** which is of God; that we might know the things that are freely given to us of God. Which things also we speak, not in the words which man's wisdom teacheth, but which the Holy Ghost teacheth; comparing spiritual things with spiritual. But the natural man receiveth not the things of the Spirit of God: for they are foolishness unto him: neither can he know them, because they are spiritually discerned. 1Corinthians 2:12-14 (KJV)*

As stated, many Christians have embraced the false belief that "soul" and "spirit" are the same thing, a doctrine taught in some churches. But Paul was careful to underscore the difference by bringing all three aspects of our nature together in a single scripture. In his letter to the church at Thessalonica, Paul wrote:

> *And the very God of peace sanctify you wholly; and I pray God your whole **spirit** and **soul** and **body** be preserved blameless unto the coming of our Lord Jesus Christ. 1 Thessalonians 5:23 (KJV)*

Some years ago, Scofield Reference Notes explained the difference between the body, soul and spirit this way:

> *Because man is **'spirit,'** he is capable of God-consciousness, and of communion with God; because he is **'soul,'** he has self-consciousness; because he is a **'body,'** he has, through his senses, world consciousness. Scofield Reference Notes (1917 Edition)*

Forever is a long, long time

Any discussion about heaven must include God's plan for getting us there. Now that we've established who and what we are in the "image" of God, let's see what God tells us about our eternal nature and what it takes to experience eternity in heaven. In the verse that is probably quoted more often than any other scripture, Jesus tells us:

For God so loved the world, that he gave his only begotten son, that whosoever believeth in him should not perish, but have everlasting life. John 3:16 (KJV)

In another well known scripture, Jesus again tells us that He is the only way to heaven:

Jesus saith unto him, I am the way, the truth, and the life: no man cometh unto the Father, but by me. John 14:6 (KJV)

And in a lesser known scripture, Jesus warned us:

He that believeth and is baptized shall be saved; but he that Believeth not shall be damned. Mark 16:16 (KJV)

Finally, Paul, the author of most of the New Testament, reinforces Jesus' words in both the Acts of the Apostles and in his letter to the Roman church:

…whosoever shall call on the name of the Lord Shall be saved. Acts 2:21, Romans 10:13 (KJV)

As we've seen, *The Bible* tells us in numerous places that the bodies of man and animal are temporary and will eventually "return to the dust" from whence they came. For example:

For that which befalleth the sons of men befalleth beasts; even one thing befalleth them: as the one dieth, so dieth the other; yea, they have all one breath; so that a man hath no preeminence above a beast: for all is vanity. Ecclesiastes 3:19 (KJV)

This means that when the writers of John, Mark, Acts, and Romans referred to "everlasting life," being "damned" and being "saved," they were not talking about our bodies. Clearly, these men were referring to the eternal aspect of our nature.

So, what have we just learned about our nature and eternity as it relates to man? Let's review some important truths:

Review

✓   God is a triune being (Father, Son, and Holy Ghost);
✓   Man was created in the "image" of God;
✓   The very essence of man is also triune (body, soul, and spirit);
✓   The spirit is that aspect of man's nature that worships God and lives forever;
✓   The soul can also live forever;
✓   We must "believe" in God's Son to have "everlasting life";
✓   Men have no other way to the Father, but by the Son;
✓   Men who don't believe in the Son will not enjoy "everlasting life."

CHAPTER THREE

WHAT DOES THE OWNER'S MANUAL TELL US ABOUT ANIMALS?

First come...first to serve

Now that we understand the nature of man, we can explore the nature of animals. Let's begin our study by looking at some of the roles God gave animals in promoting his Kingdom. The birth of Jesus is a good place to begin:

> *And she brought forth her firstborn son, and wrapped him in swaddling clothes, and laid him in a manger; because there was no room for them in the inn. Luke 2:7 (KJV)*

Isn't it amazing that the God of heaven would choose a lowly animal manger as the birthplace of His Son, the one sent to save mankind? Since mangers existed to accommodate animals, they likely were present and witnessed the birth of the Messiah. This is remarkable in that, other than Joseph and Mary, man was not among those privileged creatures. And don't forget, God didn't choose soldiers, priests, or royalty to be among the first human to see Jesus after He came into this world, but humble shepherds who were in the fields, tending their sheep:

> *And there were in the same country shepherds abiding in the field, keeping watch over their flock by night. And, lo, the angel of the Lord came upon them, and the glory of the Lord shone round about them: and they were sore afraid. And the angel said unto them, Fear not: for, behold, I bring you good tidings of great joy, which shall be to all people. For unto you is born this day in the city of David a Savior, which is Christ the Lord. And this shall be a sign unto you; Ye shall find the babe wrapped in swaddling clothes, lying in a*

manger. And suddenly there was with the angel a multitude of the heavenly host praising God, and saying, Glory to God in the highest, and on earth peace, good will toward men. And it came to pass, as the angels were gone away from them into heaven, the shepherds said one to another, Let us now go even unto Bethlehem, and see this thing which is come to pass, which the Lord hath made known unto us. And they came with haste, and found Mary, and Joseph, and the babe lying in a manger. And when they had seen it, they made known abroad the saying which was told them concerning this child. And all they that heard it wondered at those things which were told them by the shepherds. Luke 2:8-18 (KJV)

Another example of the importance God ascribes to animals is seen in the numerous references in *The Bible* wherein God's prophets use animals in a metaphorical way to help us understand the nature and mission of the coming messiah. For example, Hosea referred to him as a "lion" that would attack and destroy both sin and Satan himself:

For I will be unto Ephraim as a lion, and as a young lion to the house of Judah. Hosea 5:14 (KJV)

God wanted us to see another aspect of the mission His Son would carry out on earth by portraying him as a sacrificial "lamb," who would pay the ultimate price for the sins of mankind:

The next day John seeth Jesus coming unto him, and saith, Behold the Lamb of God, which taketh away the sin of the world. John 1:29 (KJV)

Shortly before His death on the cross, Jesus made a triumphal entry into the City of David. The Son of God could have marched into the city under escort of legions of angels. But no, God elected to make a statement about the kingdom of heaven by having Jesus enter Jerusalem on the back of a donkey, one of God's humblest creatures. This event, which was first prophesized in Zechariah 9:9, is recorded in the book of Matthew:

Tell the daughter of Zion, "Behold, your King is coming to you, Lowly, and sitting on a donkey, A colt, the foal of a donkey. Matthew 21:5 (NKJV™)

The Old Testament is full of remarkable stories wherein God used animals to promote His kingdom. For example, in what may be the most unusual story in The Bible, a donkey actually spoke to a man:

> *Now the donkey saw the Angel of the Lord standing in the way with His drawn sword in His hand, and the donkey turned aside out of the way and went into the field. So Balaam struck the donkey to turn her back onto the road. Then the Angel of the Lord stood in a narrow path between the vineyards, with a wall on this side and a wall on that side. And when the donkey saw the Angel of the Lord, she pushed herself against the wall and crushed Balaam's foot against the wall; so he struck her again. Then the Angel of the Lord went further, and stood in a narrow place where there was no way to turn either to the right hand or to the left. And when the donkey saw the Angel of the Lord, she lay down under Balaam; so Balaam's anger was aroused, and he struck the donkey with his staff. Then the Lord opened the mouth of the donkey, and she said to Balaam, "What have I done to you, that you have struck me these three times?" And Balaam said to the donkey, "Because you have abused me. I wish there were a sword in my hand, for now I would kill you!" So the donkey said to Balaam, "Am I not your donkey on which you have ridden, ever since I became yours, to this day? Was I ever disposed to do this to you?" And he said, "No." Then the Lord opened Balaam's eyes, and he saw the Angel of the Lord standing in the way with His drawn sword in His hand; and he bowed his head and fell flat on his face. And the Angel of the Lord said to him, "Why have you struck your donkey these three times? Behold, I have come out to stand against you, because your way is perverse before me. The donkey saw me and turned aside from me these three times. If she had not turned aside from me, surely I would also have killed you by now, and let her live." Numbers 22:23-33 (NKJV™)*

This passage takes on even more significance when we realize that *The Bible* does not tell us that God "opened the eyes" of the donkey, or "closed the eyes" of Balaam. It simply says the "donkey saw the angel." Does this mean the animal had a natural ability to see God's heavenly representative when the man couldn't? It's also significant that when God "opened the mouth of the donkey," the animal didn't have a message for the world or express a divine edict from God. It simply expressed its feelings and complained about being mistreated by the man whom she had faithfully served. Some would take this to mean the animal was self-aware and should, therefore, be considered more than a mere beast of burden.

The story of Jonah is a familiar, and no less amazing, example of the important roles God gives to animals. In that instance, God used a great fish to cause the wicked city of Nineveh to repent and seek God's forgiveness.

Now the Lord had prepared a great fish to swallow up Jonah. And Jonah was in the belly of the fish three days and three nights. Jonah 1:17 (KJV)

But the story of Jonah's plight had far greater significance than most would believe. Jesus referred to the incident when he told us what God's will would require of him:

For as Jonas was three days and three nights in the whale's belly; so shall the Son of man be three days and three nights in the heart of the earth. Matthew 12:40 (KJV)

Jeremiah gives us insight into some of the unique gifts God gave to animals alone, making them more perceptive than people in different ways:

Yea, the stork in the heaven knoweth her appointed times; and the turtle and the crane and the swallow observe the time of their coming; but my people know not the judgment of the Lord. Jeremiah 8:7 (KJV)

Job also tells us that animals have certain abilities that man does not possess and that we would do well to learn from them:

But ask now the beasts, and they shall teach thee; and the fowls of the air, and they shall tell thee: Or speak to the earth, and it shall teach thee: and the fishes of the sea shall declare unto thee. Who knoweth not in all these that the hand of the Lord hath wrought this? In whose hand is the soul of every living thing, and the breath of all mankind. Job 12:7-10 (KJV)

And, in another well-known story, God uses lions to teach man about faithfulness and conviction:

Then the king commanded, and they brought Daniel, and cast him into the den of lions. Now the king spake and said unto Daniel, Thy God whom thou servest continually, he will deliver thee. And a stone was brought, and laid upon the mouth of the den; and the king sealed it with his own signet, and with the signet of his Lords; that the purpose might not be changed concerning Daniel. Then the king went to his palace, and passed the night fasting: neither were instruments of music brought before him: and his sleep went from him. Then the king arose very early in the morning, and went in haste unto the den of lions. And when he came to the den, he cried with a lamentable voice unto Daniel: and the king spake and said to Daniel, O Daniel, servant of the living God, is thy God, whom thou servest continually, able to deliver thee from the lions? Then said Daniel unto the king, O king, live forever. My God hath sent his angel, and hath shut the lions' mouths, that they have not hurt me: forasmuch as before him innocency was found in me; and also before thee, O king, have I done no hurt. Then was the king exceeding glad for him, and commanded that they should take Daniel up out of the den. So Daniel was taken up out of the den, and no manner of hurt was found upon him, because he believed in his God. And the king commanded, and they brought those men which had accused Daniel, and they cast them into the den of lions, them, their children, and their wives; and the lions had the mastery of them, and brake all their bones in pieces or ever they came at the bottom of the den. Daniel 6:16-24 (KJV)

More than just a pretty face?

Animals are more than just another created "thing." Jesus told us that God loves the animals so much that He makes a point of taking care of them:

Behold the fowls of the air: for they sow not, neither do they reap, nor gather into barns; yet your heavenly Father feedeth them. Are ye not much better than they? Matthew 6:26 (KJV)

You will probably be surprised to learn that God loves animals enough to make provisions for allowing them to rest on the Sabbath:

> *But the seventh day is the sabbath of the Lord thy God: in it thou shalt not do any work, thou, nor thy son, nor thy daughter, nor thy manservant, nor thy maidservant, nor thine ox, nor thine ass, nor any of thy cattle, nor thy stranger that is within thy gates; that thy manservant and thy maidservant may rest as well as thou. Deuteronomy 5:14 (KJV)*

So why has God given us these creatures and placed them under our charge? We can never know all of the reasons, but most of us would agree that companionship is one such reason. *The Bible* supports this belief:

> *And the Lord God said, It is not good that the man should be alone; I will make him an help meet for him. And out of the ground the Lord God formed every beast of the field, and every fowl of the air; and brought them unto Adam to see what he would call them: and whatsoever Adam called every living creature, that was the name thereof. Genesis 2:18-19 (KJV)*

There are at least two other important reasons why God gave us animals. One is for the purpose of allowing them to act as substitutes for us in the sacrificial atonement for our sins. If animals weren't important to God, He never would have allowed them to die in our place, just as He did His Son:

> *And Abel, he also brought of the firstlings of his flock and of the fat thereof. And the Lord had respect unto Abel and to his offering: Genesis 4:4 (KJV)*

> *And he said, Lay not thine hand upon the lad, neither do thou any thing unto him: for now I know that thou fearest God, seeing thou hast not withheld thy son, thine only son from me. And Abraham lifted up his eyes, and looked, and behold behind him a ram caught in a thicket by his horns: and Abraham went and took the ram, and offered him up for a burnt offering in the stead of his son. Genesis 22:13-13 (KJV)*

Another reason why God gave us animals, a reason that will be clear to anyone who has ever loved a pet, is that animals are living examples of agape love. Agape, the word used by Jesus in John 13:34-35, is rarely found in ancient Greek literature. But we should not be surprised to learn that it is commonly found throughout the New Testament. Agape love does not refer to romantic or sexual love (the word "eros" does not appear in the New Testament). And, it doesn't refer to mere sentiment, a pleasant feeling or attraction to someone or something, a close friendship or brotherly attachment ("philia" in the original Greek).

When Paul wrote to the church in Corinth, he reminded the early believers how God wants us to love (agape) Him, and one another:

> *Love suffers long and is kind; love does not envy; love does not parade itself, is not puffed up; does not behave rudely, does not seek its own, is not provoked, thinks no evil; does not rejoice in iniquity, but rejoices in the truth; bears all things, believes all things, hopes all things, endures all things. Love never fails. But whether there are prophecies, they will fail; whether there are tongues, they will cease; whether there is knowledge, it will vanish away. 1 Corinthians 13:4-8 (NKJV™)*

Agape love is love that is unselfish, unconditional, and sacrificial. It is a kind of love that is given to those who are unworthy. Animals love us when we ignore or mistreat them, and don't care how much money we have in the bank. They don't care if we can play the piano or are attractive enough to land a movie contract. Animals don't sulk or deprive us of their affection when we don't give them what they want. Animals simply love us without any conditions, in spite of who and what we are. Can you think of a better example of the unconditional love we should give to one another? This, after all, is the kind of love God gives to us, and He expects us to do no less:

> *But if ye do not forgive, neither will your Father which is in heaven forgive your trespasses. Mark 11:26 (KJV)*

> *But I say unto you, Love your enemies, bless them that curse you, do good to them that hate you, and pray for them which despitefully use you, and persecute you; That ye may be the children of your Father which is in heaven: for he maketh his sun to rise on the evil and on the good, and sendeth rain on the just and on the unjust. For if ye*

love them which love you, what reward have ye? do not even the
publicans the same? Matthew 5:44-46 (KJV)

The Bible gives us many examples of animals expressing this special
form of love. Here are just two examples:

O Jerusalem, Jerusalem, which killest the prophets, and stonest them
that are sent unto thee; how often would I have gathered thy chil-
dren together, as a hen doth gather her brood under her wings, and
ye would not! Luke 13:34 (KJV)

Yea, the sparrow hath found an house, and the swallow a nest for
herself, where she may lay her young, even thine altars, O Lord of
hosts, my King, and my God. Psalms 84:3 (KJV)

Consider the nature of the beast(s)

Now that we've seen how God uses animals to proclaim His kingdom and have discussed some of the reasons He blessed us with these
creatures, let's see what He tells us about their nature. Unlike God and
man, the essence of animals is two-dimensional.

The **first** aspect of an animal's nature is the **body**. God created animals to inhabit a mortal body that decays and eventually returns to
"dust," just like that of man:

And thou mourn at the last, when thy flesh and thy BODY are con-
sumed. Proverbs 5:11 (KJV)

For that which befalleth the sons of men befalleth beasts; even one thing befalleth them: as the one dieth, so dieth the other; yea, they have all one breath; so that a man hath no preeminence above a beast: for all is vanity. Ecclesiastes 3:19 (KJV)

The Bible teaches us that the **second** (and only other) aspect of an animal's nature is the **soul**, another trait they share with man. God wanted man to know this from the beginning and addressed it in the first book of *The Bible*:

And God said, Let the waters swarm with swarmers (fish) having a living soul and let the birds fly over the earth, on the face of the expanse of the heavens. And God created the great sea animals and the creeping things all having a living soul. Genesis 1:20-21 (KJV)

And God said, Let the earth bring forth souls of life according to its kind, the cattle, the beasts of the field, and creeping things according to its kind. Genesis 1:24 (KJV)

To every animal of the earth, and to every bird of the heavens and to every creeping thing on the earth, in which is a living soul, every green plant is given for food. Genesis 1:30 (KJV)

You may be thinking that the "soul" these writers refer to is different than that which God gave to man. But no, the writer of Genesis and the Psalmist both used the same Hebrew word "nepish" (translated as "soul") when referring both to man and to animal. In the following scriptures, the exact same word for soul ("nepish) was recorded in the original Hebrew scriptures:

And God said, Let the waters swarm with swarms of living souls, and let fowl fly above the earth in the expanse of the heavens. Genesis 1:20 (Darby)

And God created the great sea monsters, and every living soul that moves with which the waters swarm, after their kind, and every winged fowl after its kind. And God saw that it was good. Genesis 1:21 (Darby)

And God said, Let the earth bring forth living souls after their kind, cattle, and creeping thing, and beast of the earth, after their kind. And it was so. Genesis 1:24 (Darby)

And to every animal of the earth, and to every fowl of the heavens, and to everything that creepeth on the earth, in which is a living soul, every green herb for food. And it was so. Genesis 1:30 (Darby)

And the Lord God formed man of the dust of the ground, and breathed into his nostrils the breath of life; and man became a living soul. Genesis 2:7 (KJV)

For thou wilt not leave my soul in hell; neither wilt thou suffer thine Holy One to see corruption. Psalms 16:10 (KJV)

Many Christians will find it difficult to accept the fact that God gave animals a soul, just as He did man. But those who choose to dismiss this Biblical truth as an impossibility, should remember what *The Bible* tells us about Holy Scripture:

All scripture is given by inspiration of God, and is profitable for doctrine, for reproof, for correction, for instruction in righteousness: 2 Timothy 3:16 (KJV)

Pet owners will agree that animals are capable of loving (and hating) humans, as well as other animals. It's a well-documented fact that animals even grieve the loss of companions, human and animal alike. Like humans, animals' feelings reside in their souls and not in their physical bodies. This means that the soul is responsible for the love exchanged between a man and an animal.

CHAPTER FOUR

OK, NOW THAT I HAVE YOUR UNDIVIDED ATTENTION.

Viva la difference!

Am I suggesting that *The Bible* tells us that man and animal are the same? Absolutely not! Remember, man is a triune creature made in the image of God (body, soul, and spirit), but animals consist only of body and soul. There can be no mistake, God never intended for us to consider animals as our equals:

All flesh is not the same flesh: but there is one kind of flesh of men, another flesh of beasts, another of fishes, and another of birds. 1 Corinthians 15:39 (KJV)

For thou hast made him a little lower than the angels, and hast crowned him with glory and honour. Thou madest him to have dominion over the works of thy hands; thou hast put all things under his feet: All sheep and oxen, yea, and the beasts of the field; The fowl of the air, and the fish of the sea, and whatsoever passeth through the paths of the seas. Psalms 8:5-8 (KJV)

And God blessed them, and God said unto them, Be fruitful, and multiply, and replenish the earth, and subdue it: and have dominion over the fish of the sea, and over the fowl of the air, and over every living thing that moveth upon the earth. Genesis 1:28 (KJV)

And, because God did not create animals with a spirit as He did man, Jesus told us that they can never experience a personal relationship with God as we can:

God is a Spirit: and they that worship him must worship him in spirit and in truth. John 4:24 (KJV)

It's also clear that, because they lack a spirit, animals cannot know the things of God:

For what man knoweth the things of a man, save the spirit of man which is in him? even so the things of God knoweth no man, but the Spirit of God. 1 Corinthains 2:11 (KJV)

That the God of our Lord Jesus Christ, the Father of glory, may give unto you the spirit of wisdom and revelation in the knowledge of him: Ephesians 1:17 (KJV)

Man and animal—a match made in heaven

Since the beginning, God's design for creation has included the existence of a close relationship between man and animal. He explains this relationship in Genesis, the first book of *The Bible*. There we learn of His covenant with man and how He made provisions for man's sustenance soon after the creation. As we've seen, Genesis tells us that God created man in His "image" and gave him "dominion" over all the animal kingdom. It also tells us that God commanded man to "be fruitful and multiply, and replenish the earth and subdue it."

Almost everyone knows man was punished for the sin he committed in the Garden and that God punished the serpent for its role in the fall of man. But many of us don't realize that animals were punished along with man. A closer look at scripture reveals that all of the other animals ("all cattle" and "every beast of the field") were also "cursed" (below that which was meted out to the serpent). Sadly, Satan tempted man in the form of an animal (serpent), and man fell into sin. Sin brought death to all of God's creation, and though animals did not commit sin (Satan only appeared as a serpent), their destiny became irrevocably linked to that of mankind:

And the Lord God said unto the serpent, Because thou hast done this, thou art cursed above all cattle, and above every beast of the field; upon thy belly shalt thou go, and dust shalt thou eat all the days of thy life: Genesis 3:14 (KJV)

We know that as a result of the original sin, death became the destiny of man. But it was the animals that were the first to taste death after God killed them in order to make clothing out of their skins for Adam and Eve:

> *Unto Adam also and to his wife did the Lord God make coats of skins, and clothed them. Genesis 3:21 (KJV)*

Most of us don't really understand how closely the destinies of man and animal are linked. For example, did you know that when God killed the firstborn in the land of Egypt (during the "Passover"), he did not make an exception for the animals?

> *And all the firstborn in the land of Egypt shall die, from the firstborn of Pharaoh that sitteth upon his throne, even unto the firstborn of the maidservant that is behind the mill; and all the firstborn of beasts. Exodous 11:5 (KJV)*

The Bible reveals other instances where the destiny of animals was linked to that of man. A notable example occurred during the time of Noah. God's reaction to man's ever-increasing indulgence in wickedness and depravity was to punish both man and "beast" alike:

> *And God saw that the wickedness of man was great in the earth, and that every imagination of the thoughts of his heart was only evil continually. And it repented the Lord that he had made man on the earth, and it grieved him at his heart. And the Lord said, I will destroy man whom I have created from the face of the earth; both man, and beast, and the creeping thing, and the fowls of the air; for it repenteth me that I have made them. But Noah found grace in the eyes of the Lord. Genesis 6:5-8 (KJV)*

But God gave His creation a second chance. He told Noah (the only man who "found grace in the eyes of the Lord") that He would establish a new covenant with him, his family and "every living creature of all flesh that is upon the earth." Once again, the destiny of the animals was to be the same as man's:

> *And, behold, I, even I, do bring a flood of waters upon the earth, to destroy all flesh, wherein is the breath of life, from under heaven; and*

every thing that is in the earth shall die. But with thee will I establish my covenant; and thou shalt come into the ark, thou, and thy sons, and thy wife, and thy sons' wives with thee. Genesis 6:17-18 (KJV)

And it shall come to pass, when I bring a cloud over the earth, that the bow shall be seen in the cloud: And I will remember my covenant, which is between me and you and every living creature of all flesh; and the waters shall no more become a flood to destroy all flesh. And the bow shall be in the cloud; and I will look upon it, that I may remember the everlasting covenant between God and every living creature of all flesh that is upon the earth. And God said unto Noah, This is the token of the covenant, which I have established between me and all flesh that is upon the earth Genesis 9:9-17 (KJV)

Because of Adam, all of creation, including the animals, was cursed and made subject to death. But as a result of God's covenant with Noah, every living creature was given the possibility of a reprieve. But what exactly did God's covenant include? It gave man another opportunity to seek redemption and be reconciled to God. Since this covenant included "every living creature," did God extend the possibility of eternal life to the animals as well?

Before we see how God's word answers these questions, we must recognize that God's word tells us that some men will never gain redemption. As we've read, belief in Jesus and his sacrificial, atoning death on the cross is necessary for everlasting life. Those who choose to reject this gift will be condemned.

Nothing less than a sincere belief will be acceptable to God, and Jesus warned us that it is not enough to simply "talk the talk" without "walking the walk." Read Jesus' warning as recorded in the book of Matthew:

Not every one that saith unto me, Lord, Lord, shall enter into the kingdom of heaven; Matthew 7:21 (KJV)

CHAPTER FIVE

BUT YOU CAN'T GET THERE FROM HERE...OR CAN YOU?

Not just another four-letter word

Jesus wants us to know that the target of God's love is the entire "world" which, by definition, includes the animals:

For God so loved the world..." John 3:16 (KJV)

There can be no mistake, God loves the animals and He wants them to love him as well:

Praise the Lord from the earth, ye dragons, and all deeps: Beasts, and all cattle; creeping things, and flying fowl: Psalms 148:7, 10 (KJV)

Furthermore, God wants man to love animals, just as He loves us:

A righteous man regardeth the life of his beast: but the tender mercies of the wicked are cruel. Proverbs 12:10 (KJV)

Remember, *The Bible* tells us that man's essence is three-dimensional in nature (body, soul and spirit), while God's Word tells us that the essence of animals is only two-dimensional (body and soul). It is our spirit that distinguishes us from the animals. We've read that the things of God must be discerned spiritually (1 Corinthians 2:14), including the fact that God is a spirit and must be worshiped "in spirit" (John 4:24).

In order to understand how animals, who don't have a spirit, could possibly enter into heaven, we must explore another important fundamental in God's plan for his creation, the blessed gift of love. To put the importance of love into perspective, Jesus told us that God is not only "spirit," but "love" as well:

And we have known and believed the love that God hath to us. God is love; and he that dwelleth in love dwelleth in God, and God in him. 1 John 4:16 (KJV)

Paul stresses the importance of love, telling us that it is even "greater" than faith and hope. Read what he wrote to the church at Corinth:

Though I speak with the tongues of men and of angels, but have not love, I have become sounding brass or a clanging cymbal. And though I have the gift of prophecy, and understand all mysteries and all knowledge, and though I have all faith, so that I could remove mountains, but have not love, I am nothing. And though I bestow all my goods to feed the poor, and though I give my body to be burned, but have not love, it profits me nothing. Love suffers long and is kind; love does not envy; love does not parade itself, is not puffed up; does not behave rudely, does not seek its own, is not provoked, thinks no evil; does not rejoice in iniquity, but rejoices in the truth; bears all things, believes all things, hopes all things, endures all things. Love never fails. 1 Corinthians 13:1-10 (NKJV™)

And now these three remain: faith, hope and love. But the greatest of these is love. 1 Corinthians 13:13 (NKJV™)

But above all these things put on love, which is the bond of perfection. Colossians 3:14 (NKJV™)

Peter had a lot to say about love as well, and even made the profound statement that love can be "an entrance into the everlasting kingdom of our Lord and Savior Jesus Christ:"

But also for this very reason, giving all diligence, add to your faith virtue, to virtue knowledge, to knowledge self-control, to self-control perseverance, to perseverance godliness, to godliness brotherly kindness, and to brotherly kindness love. For if these things are yours and abound, you will be neither barren nor unfruitful in the knowledge of our Lord Jesus Christ. For he who lacks these things is shortsighted, even to blindness, and has forgotten that he was cleansed from his old sins. Therefore, brethren, be even more diligent to make your call and election sure, for if you do these things you will never stumble; for so an entrance will be supplied to you abundantly into the everlasting kingdom of our Lord and Savior Jesus Christ. 2 Peter 1:5-11 (NKJV™)

Playing for keeps

In this age of hyper-sensitivity, many people choose to practice revisionist theology in order to be "politically correct." But the fact remains that when a man chooses to shun God's gift of "eternal life," he is damned to an eternal "death" (including separation from God) in hell:

For the wages of sin is death; but the gift of God is eternal life through Jesus Christ our Lord. Romans 6:23 (KJV)

For to be carnally minded is death; but to be spiritually minded is life and peace. Romans 8:6 (KJV)

Then when lust hath conceived, it bringeth forth sin: and sin, when it is finished, bringeth forth death. James 1:15 (KJV)

But the fearful, and unbelieving, and the abominable, and murderers, and whoremongers, and sorcerers, and idolaters, and all liars, shall have their part in the lake which burneth with fire and brimstone: which is the second death. Revelations 21:8 (KJV)

We've also learned that the bodies of all men return to dust when they die. And, in the book of Matthew, Jesus tells us the souls of those who die in their sins will also be "destroyed" in hell:

And fear not them which kill the body, but are not able to kill the soul: but rather fear him which is able to destroy both soul and body in hell. Matthew 10:28 (KJV)

We read in 1 Kings 17:21-22 that a soul can be delivered from death, and the Psalmist affirms that a soul can be saved from destruction:

But God will redeem my Soul from the power of the grave: for he shall receive me. Psalms 49:15 (KJV)

For thou hast delivered my Soul from death, mine eyes from tears, and my feet from falling. Psalms 116:8 (KJV)

But what about the animals? If animals are sinless and do not go to hell, which is reserved for Satan, his angels, and sinful man, what happens to them when they die? *The Bible* tells us the bodies of animals return to dust, like those of men, but it doesn't tell us what happens to their souls. Or, does it? Remember, Psalms 49:15, Psalms 116:8, and 1 Kings 17:21-22 all tell us a soul can be eternal. John provides evidence of this fact when he describes a glimpse of redeemed "souls" in his vision of heaven:

And I saw thrones, and they sat upon them, and judgment was given unto them: and I saw the souls of them that were beheaded for the witness of Jesus, and for the word of God, and which had not worshipped the beast, neither his image, neither had received his mark upon their foreheads, or in their hands; and they lived and reigned with Christ a thousand years. Revelations 20:4 (KJV)

James gives us yet another affirmation that a soul can be saved from death:

Let him know, that he which converteth the sinner from the error of his way shall save a soul from death and shall hide a multitude of sins. James 5:20 (KJV)

Souls have another characteristic that is relevant to our study. *The Bible* tells us they are capable of **LOVING**:

And it came to pass, when he had made an end of speaking unto Saul, that the Soul of Jonathan was knit with the Soul of David, and Jonathan loved him as his own Soul. 1 Samuel 18:1 (KJV)

And thou shalt love the Lord thy God with all thy heart, and with all thy Soul, and with all thy mind, and with all thy strength: this is the first commandment. Mark 12:30 (KJV)

We know that, unlike man, animals do not go to hell, so it follows that their souls cannot be destroyed there. So what happens to an animal's soul when the creature dies? Since animals don't have a spirit and cannot choose to be redeemed, do their souls simply cease to exist? The answer to this question is, *yes* for some, and *no* for others.

Allow me to show you to the door

Jesus told us that God did not restrict the gift of salvation to man, but intended it for *"all flesh"* which, therefore, includes the animals:

> And all flesh shall see the salvation of God. Luke 3:6 (KJV)

In his letter to the Roman church, Paul stressed that God made provisions for animals in His plan for eternal life:

> For the creation was subjected to futility, not willingly, but because of Him who subjected it in hope; because the creation itself also will be delivered from the bondage of corruption into the glorious liberty of the children of God. For we know that the whole creation groans and labors with birth pangs together until now. Not only that, but we also who have the firstfruits of the Spirit, even we ourselves groan within ourselves, eagerly waiting for the adoption, the redemption of our body. Romans 8:20-23 (NKJV™)

Paul told the Roman church that Jesus will deliver "all of creation" from the certainty of "bondage" (or death) which is the end of the "corruptible" (or temporary) bodies we currently inhabit. But, if *The Bible* tells us there is a doorway through which animals can enter, how do they pass through that door?

And here's the key to that door

> ...for so an entrance will be supplied to you abundantly into the everlasting kingdom of our Lord and Savior Jesus Christ. 2 Peter 1:11 (NKJV™)

ut, **LOVE** is the key to understanding God's will for ani-
...e key that unlocks the door to eternal life. It is the bridge
...at allows animals to cross into God's heavenly realm. How can this
be? *The Bible* tells us that love is forever and will live as long as the loving creature exists. Solomon, the wisest man who ever lived, explains
the nature of love:

> *Set me as a seal upon thine heart, as a seal upon thine arm: for love*
> *is strong as death; jealousy is cruel as the grave: the coals thereof are*
> *coals of fire, which hath a most vehement flame. Many waters can-*
> *not quench love, neither can the floods drown it: if a man would give*
> *all the substance of his house for love, it would utterly be con-*
> *temned. Song of Solomon 8:6-7 (KJV)*

Note that Solomon did not say the "love of God" or the "love for one
another," he simply said "love." Anyone who has ever loved a pet knows
that such love is as real as the love we feel for other humans. And, there is
no doubt that the love our pets feel towards us is no less authentic or profound. When viewed in the greater context, The Bible tells us that bodily
death cannot destroy love because it will live on in the redeemed who
will enjoy "eternal life." But when man chooses to reject redemption
through Jesus Christ, he succumbs to eternal "death" and love cannot
exist independent of the creature. One way to understand this is to consider a memory. Memories can live forever, but only as long as the host
creature exists. If there is no creature, there can be no memory. Likewise,
if there is no host creature, there can be no love.

If the spirit of redeemed man is blessed with "eternal life" (in
heaven), what happens to the "eternal" love that he shared with a
beloved pet? Would a just God allow man and the love he had for an
animal to live forever, while depriving him of that sinless animal's
companionship for all time? It is the "unquenchable" love that is
"strong as death" that bridges the gap between the cessation of existence for the animal and eternal life at man's side.

When man receives the gift of "eternal life" by way of God's Son,
the love he has for an animal cannot die, and will continue to exist
within his eternal soul and spirit. The "eternal" love an animal shares
with a redeemed man will continue to live on in its "eternal" soul as
well. Not because the man has the power or ability to give such a gift to
the animal, but because God's grace has linked the destiny of animals
to that of man by means of love, His greatest gift.

By His grace, God allows the triune man, created in His "image," to share the gift of love with the two-dimensional animal. At death, the bodies of both creatures return to the dust from whence they came. But the soul and spirit of a redeemed man, as well as the soul of the animal that loved him, carry on in heaven in a loving relationship that will never die. The love shared between an animal and a redeemed man will sustain the animal's soul in eternity.

It takes two, baby!

What about the animals that love, and are loved by, men who die in their sins? *The Bible* tells us that animals don't have an eternal spirit, but they do have a soul. This is important because, as we've read, *The Bible* also says there are souls in heaven, which means they can be "eternal" as well. So, if God's word tells us that the love an animal shares with a redeemed man makes it possible for the soul of that creature to enter into heaven, what happens to the animals who love, and are loved by, men who have chosen eternal "death" over redemption?

The Bible tells us that the body of the animal returns to dust. And since hell, where body and soul are "destroyed," is reserved for Satan, his angels, and sinful man, we can only conclude that the souls of the animals who loved sinful men will return to their former state of nonexistence. Remember, if there is no creature, there can be no love. And, if there is no mutual love between a man and an animal, there is no doorway that will allow animals to enter into heaven.

Does this seem cruel and unfair? Remember, God's word tells us that there will be many men, all created in His "image," who will reject God and therefore be denied the gift of "eternal life." So, we should not be surprised or disheartened to learn that, since the destiny of animals is linked to that of man, many of them will also be denied the blessed gift of eternal life.

The relationship between man and animal exists in one of three states of existence: in life; in death; and in eternity. The following shows those relationships in a graphic format:

THE RELATIONSHIP AS IT EXISTS IN LIFE

AS IT EXISTS AT DEATH

AS IT WILL EXIST FOR THE REDEEMED

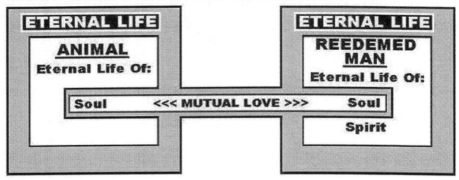

So there you have it…in the end, the destiny of animals is linked to that of man one last time.

CHAPTER SIX

DON'T TURN THE LIGHTS OUT YET–THERE'S MORE

Behold, the *coup de grâce*

Given the controversial nature of this topic, there will always be skeptics. Those individuals would do well to consider the fact that *The Bible* not only tells us animals can enjoy eternal life, it even gives specific examples of the role some will play in the advent of God's kingdom. These are not "horses of fire," but just simple animals. Read the words of the prophets Isaiah and Hosea:

> *The wolf also shall dwell with the lamb, and the leopard shall lie down with the kid; and the calf and the young lion and the fatling together; and a little child shall lead them. And the cow and the bear shall feed; their young ones shall lie down together: and the lion shall eat straw like the ox. And the sucking child shall play on the hole of the asp, and the weaned child shall put his hand on the cockatrice' den. Isaiah 11:6-8 (KJV)*

> *"Then I will make a covenant on behalf of Israel with the wild beasts, the birds of the air, and the things that creep on the earth, and I will break bow and sword and weapon of war and sweep them off the earth, so that all living creatures may lie down without fear" (Hosea 2:18) (KJV)*

> *And I saw an angel standing in the sun; and he cried with a loud voice, saying to all the fowls that fly in the midst of heaven, Come and gather yourselves together unto the supper of the great God; Revelation 19:17 (KJV)*

And it came to pass, as they still went on, and talked, that, behold, there appeared a chariot of fire, and horses of fire, and parted them both asunder; and Elijah went up by a whirlwind into heaven. 2 Kings 2:11 (KJV)

Let's throw in one more biblical truth for good measure

Over the years, many people have asked me what we will look like in heaven. *The Bible* tells us that our bodies will be "raised" as "spiritual bodies:"

It is sown a natural body; it is raised a spiritual body. There is a natural body, and there is a spiritual body. 1 Corinthians 15:44 (KJV)

So what does this mean? Popular myth would have us believe that we'll sprout wings, acquire a halo and learn to strum a harp. But as is often the case, *The Bible* does not support this belief. The concept of "spirit" bodies is one we likely will not understand until we take our place in the Kingdom of God. But one thing we do know for certain is that we will "know" others and others will "know" us:

For now we see through a glass, darkly; but then face to face; now I know in part; but then I shall know [fully] even as also I am known. 1 Corinthians 13:12 (KJV)

This scripture tells us that all those in heaven will "know" and be "known." This can only mean that we will know our pets and they will know us.

And if I'm wrong?

What happens if we choose to believe that pets can go to heaven, but it turns out that such is not the case? Does this mean we've committed blasphemy or some other damnable sin? Will we be forbidden from passing "Go" and doomed to go straight to hell without "collecting $200?" No, this belief is not relevant to our salvation. As I said in the

Introduction, believing it won't get us to heaven, and disbelieving will not send us to hell. I'm convinced that God will not condemn us as long as we pursue the meaning of His word with sincerity while remaining faithful to His plan for the salvation of mankind.

Because of man's initial "fall" in the Garden, we have all been cursed with an imperfect nature and are destined to fail on occasion. But God looks upon the heart and forgives us when we err in "good faith," especially when His will for us is subject to different interpretations. If this were not true, entire denominations would be condemned to hell. But this does not mean we are at liberty to believe anything we want. *The Bible* gives us concise mandates about certain beliefs and practices. For example, God's word condemns the worship of animals, idols, and false gods. So such a practice would be sinful, even if done in "good faith."

As you've read, God answers our questions about animals and their eternal destination. I believe he tells us that some animals will exist in eternity at the side of the redeemed people they loved. But even if I'm mistaken, I can take comfort in knowing we will not suffer without them. Paul gives us this assurance in his letter to the church in Corinth:

> *But as it is written, eye hath not seen, nor ear heard, neither have entered into the heart of man, the things which God hath prepared for them that love him. I Corinthians 2:9 (KJV)*

But even more to the point, John wrote:

> *And God shall wipe away all tears from their eyes; and there shall be no more death, neither sorrow, nor crying, neither shall there be any more pain: for the former things are passed away. Revelations 21:4 (KJV)*

Let's do the math

McClinton's Perpetual Pet Postulate (P_3): Baise Pascal, a French mathematician, physicist, philosopher, and theologian who lived from 1623-1662 is best known for his "wager." Pascal, a Christian believer and apologist, argued that while God's existence cannot be known with rational certainty, it is nevertheless prudent to believe in God. In his book, *Pensées*, Pascal argued that either God exists, or He does not exist. However, our present life and our future destiny rest upon which

conclusion we choose. Pascal reasoned that by believing in G
(Christian theism), you have everything to win (eternal life), and nothing to lose. However, by not believing, you have nothing to win, and
everything to lose ("eternal death"). He, therefore, reasoned that the
best, or safest, wager is to believe in God. Another way to look at
Pascal's Wager is as follows:

> *If I believe and God exists: I'll be happy for eternity, so,. infinite gain*
> = **WIN**
> *If I believe and God does not exist: I've lost nothing* = **WIN**

But…

> *If I do not believe and God exists: I'll be punished for eternity, so,*
> *infinite loss* = **LOSE**
> *If I do not believe and God does not exist: I've lost nothing* = **WIN**

By using Pascal's Wager as a starting point, I've created McClinton's
Perpetual Pet Postulate (P_3), a tool that can be used to help us answer
the question of whether or not animals go to heaven:

> *If I believe they will, and I'm right:*
> *I'm happy now in this life and in eternity as well* = **WIN/WIN**

> *If I believe they will, and I'm wrong:*
> *I'm happy now and will still be happy in eternity because there is no*
> *pain or suffering in heaven* = **WIN/WIN**

But…

> *If I don't believe they will, and I'm right:*
> *I'm not happy now, but will still be happy in eternity because there*
> *is no pain or suffering*
> *in heaven* = **LOSE/WIN**

> *If I don't believe they will, and I'm wrong:*
> *I'm not happy now, but will still be happy in eternity because there*
> *is no pain or suffering*
> *in heaven* = **LOSE/WIN**

The way I "calculate" it, believing that *The Bible* tells us that some
pets will go to heaven represents the best possible ("WIN/WIN")
proposition. How do you choose to figure it?

The bottom line

o find a short, one-line answer in *The Bible* that _..on of whether or not pets go to heaven, you may be .ppointed. But as stated, *The Bible* gives us the answer; we only have to seek it with a sincere, prayerful spirit. Those individuals who feel God's judgment may be too harsh, or that eternal life should be given without any strings attached, would do well to remember the subtle reminder Abraham gave God so long ago:

Shall not the Judge of all the earth do right? Genesis 18:25 (KJV)

Knowing this to be true, we can be at peace in this present life. Heed the words of Paul as he encouraged us to be on guard against allowing Satan to draw us into a destructive cycle of worry over needless doubts and fears:

Finally, brethren, whatsoever things are true, whatsoever things are honest, whatsoever things are just, whatsoever things are pure, whatsoever things are lovely, whatsoever things are of good report; if there be any virtue, and if there be any praise, think on these things. Philippians 4:8 (KJV)

Let's summarize what we've learned

We've covered a lot of territory and I'm glad you "endured unto the end." Now let's go back and summarize what we've discovered:

- ✓ God created man in his image and gave him dominion over the animals;
- ✓ God gave us the animals for companionship and as an example of his unconditional love for us;
- ✓ Having been created in the "image" of God, man's very essence is triune in nature: body, soul, and spirit;
- ✓ The spirit is that aspect of man's nature that worships God and lives forever;
- ✓ There are souls in heaven so we know they also live forever;
- ✓ The essence of animals is dual in nature: body and soul;

- ✓ Because man was blessed with a spirit, he was given free choice and the option of accepting God's plan for "everlasting life";
- ✓ Animals were not given the ability to accept Jesus as the savior of the world;
- ✓ Man's spirit is "stronger" than death and can live eternally;
- ✓ God tells us that love is the "greatest" of all his gifts and that love will never die;
- ✓ The destiny of animals is linked to that of man;
- ✓ *The Bible* tells us that "all creation" can be delivered from the bonds of death, and even gives us examples of animals in heaven;
- ✓ The love between an animal and a man will exist in heaven if the man accepts God's gift of "eternal life";
- ✓ Love bridges the gap for the animal who shares a mutual love with a redeemed man;
- ✓ The soul of that animal will live in eternity along with the human(s) it loved;
- ✓ Sadly, some men will not make it to heaven–and some animals won't either;
- ✓ The body and soul of sinful man are destroyed in hell;
- ✓ The soul of an animal is not destroyed in hell, because hell is reserved for Satan, his angels, and sinful man;
- ✓ If a man is damned to everlasting "death," than the animal that loved him will simply revert to its former state of non-existence;
- ✓ Acceptance of this Biblical belief represents a win/win proposition for mankind.

Will there be paw prints in heaven?
Yes, by the grace of God.

Because it's there
Jim McClinton

I can't see it or hear it but it's there.
I can't touch it or smell it but it's there.

It makes me laugh, it make me cry because it's there.
It makes my life worth living because it's there.

A heavy cloud obscures my heart, because it's there.
But sunbeams peak through and warm my soul, because it's there

You're no longer here with me, but still, it's there.
And though our walk together had ended, still, it's there.

My sorrow will soon turn to joy, because it's there.
And I know I'll be just fine, because it's there.

So I choose to cry no longer, because it's there.
And will celebrate the life we shared, because it's there.

As I watch the years pass before my eyes, it will be there.
And though my memories may grow dim, it will be there.

But for now, I can sing and laugh again, because it's there.
And enjoy a summer breeze again, because it's there.

The flowers smell so sweet again, because it's there.
A warm gentle rain is a blessing once again, because it's there.

I know your absence is only for a season, because it's there.
And that God will bring us back together, because it's there.

And when it's time for me to leave, it will be there.
As I go to be with the Father, it will be there.

When you and I are reunited, it will be there.
And with you at my side again, it will be there.

As we enjoy God's gifts forever, it will be there.
The gift of love from Heaven above, will always be there.

Christians and Pet Loss

PART TWO

CHAPTER SEVEN

TO EVERYTHING THERE IS A SEASON

Facing the facts of life...and death

"Heaven goes by favor. If it went by merit,
you would stay out and your dog would go in."
—Mark Twain

Sooner or later, we have to face the painful truth that our pets are going to die. This sad reality becomes obvious to us when our pets are terminally ill or are unable to function because of pain that cannot be relieved. We do not have the power to choose whether or not our pets will die, but we can decide how and when. In making that decision, the fundamental consideration should be how much pain and suffering we want them to endure.

Most of us can't help but wonder how we will know when our pets are suffering, or when it may be time to "put them to sleep." It can be difficult to distinguish changes in behavior that are the result of aging from those that can be attributed to pain and suffering. A loss in the quality of life is an expected consequence of the aging process and since our pets can't speak to us, it may be difficult to know just how serious a pet's condition is.

As most of us know, aging pets become less active and seem to want to spend most of their time sleeping. That little companion who used to love playing tug-of-war with you or wanted to chase after the stick you tossed may lose interest as it gets older. In many instances, an animal's body weight may stay the same, but its appetite may decrease and it may even lose interest in that special treat. Many will experience arthritis, a stiffening of joints, or a weakening of their muscles. A loss of vision and hearing is experienced by many animals as they age. These are all normal indications and probably nothing to be concerned about.

When animals are in pain, they often exhibit sudden changes in stamina, activity level, behavior, and in the way they react to familiar people in their lives. You may notice that food dishes are left untouched due to a lack of appetite. Some animals may display their condition by changes in expression, or in the way they appear to perceive their surroundings. They may not care to move, or be moved, and have no interest in playing or going for walks. Unlike people, most animals suffer in silence. But some will whimper or cry when the pain is bad enough.

Having a pet is one of life's greatest blessings and, one of its biggest responsibilities as well. The day-to-day problems can be challenging enough, but nothing compares to the difficulty of coping with the problems that come at the end of a pet's life. The sad reality is that the life span of our pets is almost always shorter than our own. Very few animals will die quietly in their sleep, and many pass away after a lot of pain and suffering. Some of us will lose our pets after a long and painful decline, while others will lose their beloved companions suddenly and unexpectedly. Regardless, most of us are not prepared for the pain and sorrow that accompanies the death of a pet. It is only then that we begin to realize how much they contribute to our lives.

It may not seem like it, but the greatest gift of love we can give our pets is the decision to bring their suffering to an end peacefully and quietly. Imagine the relief it can give to an animal that is sick or so badly injured that every moment of its life is filled with unceasing excruciating pain. In many instances where the quality of life is nothing less than horrific for a suffering animal, euthanasia is a kind and humane way to give it the peace it longs for. Still, whether or not to euthanize is one of the most difficult decisions we will ever have to face.

Euthanization is almost always the right decision. Ironically, many people make the mistake of waiting too long to arrive at that conclusion. Those who put it off until their pets are in extremis, are forced to consider the option at a time when they're under a lot of stress and are dealing with conflicting emotions about what's best for their pet. Some pet owners feel that euthanization is a selfish act. But in reality, the exact opposite is true. No matter how well intended, waiting until the last moment is actually the ultimate act of selfishness because it forces the pet to endure needless suffering. Ironically, many people regret having waited so long and even feel guilty after finally realizing that euthanasia would have been the best course of action for their pet's sake.

Making the decision even more difficult is the fact that you may have to determine how much medical treatment to pursue. Will continued treatment only prolong the suffering and add to the pet's trauma? Medical treatments can be very expensive and are not covered by insurance so you will ultimately have to ask yourself how much you can afford. Are you capable of giving the animal the special care it will need, especially if you work and can't be with it during the day? Circumstances are often such that you have only hours or minutes to ponder these and other such issues. This is why you should look ahead and do the necessary research now. It is so much better for all involved when you have contingency plans in place for when the time comes.

Our pets depend on us for everything through the years and learn to trust the decisions we make on their behalf. That must include the decision to allow them to die in peace with grace and dignity. Failure to do so only prolongs an animal's suffering unnecessarily. By waiting until it can no longer eat or get around, we show that we are more concerned about our own sense of loss than the animal's welfare.

Thinking the unthinkable

"I think dogs were put in this world to remind humanity that love, loyalty, devotion, courage, patience, and good humor are qualities that, with honesty, are the essence of admirable character and the very definition of a life well lived."
—Dean Koontz

What exactly is euthanasia? Is it a form of lethal injection? With respect to animals, euthanasia is typically accomplished by means of an intravenous injection of a concentrated dose of anesthetic. Most animals have had injections before and are not traumatized by the needle. The injected solution normally takes mere seconds to bring about a total loss of consciousness and the animal goes into a quiet and irreversible deep unconsciousness. Soon afterwards, the animal's respiratory system is depressed and this is followed by cardiac arrest. The whole process normally takes 2-3 minutes. "Putting an animal to sleep" is an accurate way to describe this painless method of ending its suffering.

It is difficult to see a beloved pet suffer and we feel absolutely helpless as our hearts struggle against our brains while we try to determine what's best for our pets. This leads to stress that can manifest itself in many different ways. Some pet owners are stunned to find themselves angry at their pets for forcing them to make such a profound decision. Others simply cannot accept the reality of the situation and try to convince themselves that "things will be better in the morning." Guilt can complicate the process if we allow ourselves to believe there is something wrong with us for even considering euthanasia. To make matters worse, many of us will oscillate between all of these states.

The prolonged suffering of a family pet may be a burden that you and your family may not be able to bear emotionally or financially. But in the end, we all must answer the fundamental question of what's best for our pet. Deciding to euthanize does not mitigate our sorrow, but it does eliminate the guilt that results from waiting too long to decide. It also brings us relief when we see that our pet is no longer suffering in a horrendous way.

Family members should be consulted when appropriate and given the opportunity to express their feelings. Encourage them to express their thoughts and feelings, even if you have already reached a decision. Children have special relationships with their pets and they should not be excluded or protected from the decision-making process unless they are too young or too frail emotionally. Denying them the opportunity to express their feelings may only complicate their grieving and cause additional problems. Children can handle answers to difficult questions when presented in a manner that is simple, straightforward, and honest. If properly explained, the death of a pet can be understood by most children.

When you find yourself in a position of being forced to make the "final" decision on behalf of your pet, you should ask yourself the following questions:

- ✓ Is my pet interested in its surroundings or even aware of them?
- ✓ Is my pet in pain?
- ✓ Is my pet still playful? Is it eating well? Does it show me any affection?
- ✓ Does my pet seem tired and withdrawn most of the time?
- ✓ Has my pet become vicious, dangerous, or unmanageable?
- ✓ Does it "yip" or cry excessively because it is in constant pain?
- ✓ Has my pet become anorexic or lethargic?
- ✓ Is there anything I can do to give my pet relief or make it more comfortable?
- ✓ Has treatment and training failed to alter my pet's undesirable or abnormal behavior?

- ✓ Are there any other treatment options I can pursue?
- ✓ Has blindness, increasing dementia, uncontrollable incontinence, immobility, or intense pain forced me to isolate my pet?
- ✓ Am I prevented from giving my pet the love and companionship it needs because of its condition?
- ✓ Have I become angry or resentful because of the impact its condition has on my lifestyle?
- ✓ Do I think my pet senses my resentment or withdrawal?
- ✓ What is the current quality of my pet's life and is it likely to change?
- ✓ Am I capable of handling the emotional or financial burden?

Don't try to sort it all out by yourself

"To err is human—to forgive, canine."
—Anonymous

It is critical that you establish a good relationship with a veterinarian you trust. When you start to see telltale symptoms, especially if your pet is older, you need to move quickly and do as much as possible to determine what is happening. There are a number of tests a vet can perform that will not induce stress in your pet. This can be important when dealing with an animal that is already traumatized. Non-invasive tests such as radiographs, ultrasounds, and blood tests are simple and relatively painless, and they can reveal critical diagnostic information. But in the final analysis, you will have to rely on your veterinarian's opinion when deciding which procedures are necessary and in the animal's best interest.

Your veterinarian is your greatest ally when the situation is such that you feel you have to consider euthanasia. He or she not only understands your attachment to your pet, but can also make an objective assessment of your pet's condition, give you a good prognosis of its chances for recovery, and discuss quality of life issues, such as disabilities and long-term problems. Your veterinarian can explain the medical options, but he or she cannot make the final decision to euthanize. That is your responsibility and no one else's.

At first glance, the fact that veterinarians are willing to euthanize animals may appear to be contrary to their commitment to helping them. It may seem odd that they devote many years to getting a medical education in order to help animals, only to be willing to end the lives of some of those same animals. You can rest assured however, that veterinary professionals understand the balance between life and life with suffering, and are willing to exercise the ultimate gift of compassion and mercy. This is absolutely consistent with their commitment to ensuring quality of life for the animals they love.

When evaluating your pet's situation, you *must* be as fair, objective, and unselfish as possible. There are no easy answers, and there is very little you can do to avoid the pain you'll experience after your pet is gone. But prolonging your pet's suffering because it is too painful to see it die is anything but an act of love and must be avoided.

As you consider the facts, it's absolutely essential that you fully understand your pet's condition. This means you have to ask the doctor to explain every aspect of your pet's diagnosis and what it means to the animal's future. You will want to know what symptoms to expect as your pet's condition worsens and the stages it will pass through. You will also want to know when to expect incontinence or renal failure. Will the disease spread into other organs and if so, what should you expect next? When will your pet no longer be able to function normally or be overcome by pain and suffering? Finally, you will want to know how long it will be before the symptoms become medically unmanageable or the pain becomes so severe it is no longer treatable. Remember, if you're not satisfied with the way your veterinarian addresses these concerns, there is nothing wrong with seeking a second opinion, as long as the resultant delay does not cause your pet to endure unnecessary suffering.

Once you know what to expect, you should focus on developing a plan that includes milestones or action triggers. This means, for example, that you'll begin to consider euthanasia when your pet can no longer eat, drink, or even breathe without putting forth considerable effort. The trigger might be your realization that your pet can no longer find a comfortable position to sleep, or cannot be touched without experiencing pain. Thinking matters through while you're still able to think calmly and rationally makes it so much easier to make the best decisions and to do what is best for your pet.

Knowing when the time has come

"If cats could talk, they wouldn't."
—Nan Porter

Our pets live simple lives and need little to be content. When a pet is terminally ill, critically injured, or has reached the stage in its life where it can no longer do the little things that once meant so much, it may be time to consider euthanasia. If a pet does not respond to affection, seems unaware or uninterested in its surroundings, or is undergoing difficult and stressful treatments that aren't helping, then it may be time to give the animal the relief it deserves. When constant pain and suffering becomes a pet's lifestyle, we need to seriously consider doing the only thing that will give bring the relief it longs for.

You may have heard that our pets will let us know when it's time to leave us by giving some sort of signal exhibiting a quirk in behavior that we can readily identify. That would be wonderful, if it were true. Unfortunately, most of us never receive such a signal and probably couldn't discern it even if it were given. By believing our pets will let us know when it's time to die, we are probably only prolonging their suffering and it's likely we will eventually experience guilt when we realize what we've done.

Some pet owners refuse to consider euthanasia because they feel it is not nature's way. These individuals believe every creature has its own appointed time and manner in which to die, and the act of ending their lives artificially is contrary to nature's timetable. Yet, those same individuals see nothing wrong with taking their pets in for medication, treatment, or surgery. Such actions are also "artificial" and since they can extend the life of a pet, could also be considered "contrary to nature's timetable." The bottom line is, we should always do whatever is best for our pets.

Saying goodbye

"Every dog has his day."
—Miguel de Cervantes

An important step in coming to terms with the loss of your pet is the act of saying goodbye. Pet owners who lose a pet will face the immediate onslaught of a number of different feelings including grief, sorrow, anger and loneliness. Those who miss the opportunity to bid farewell to their loving companions will probably find themselves dealing with feelings of regret and guilt, as well. Hopefully, most people will be able to spend a final night at home with their pet or say goodbye at the clinic. Most vets are happy to accommodate those who ask to spend time alone with their animal at the end.

Once the decision is made, it's a good idea to talk to your pet about it, explaining you are making a decision to end the pain and suffering. Our pets love it when we talk to them, especially at a time such as this. Tell your pet you love it dearly and will always remember it as an important member of your family. If you can bring yourself to do it, hold your pet while it is put to sleep. This final act will be the most precious gift you ever give yourself, and your pet as well. That moment will live on forever and your pet's final moments on this earth will be immersed in the totality of your love.

Finally, as a Christian, you should pray with your pet. Your pet will appreciate your presence and sense the peace that comes from the prayer. God will surely honor your prayer and give your pet the rest you both seek.

CHAPTER EIGHT

AND NOW THE HARD PART

Should you be present during euthanasia?

"A dog is the only thing on this earth that loves you
more than he loves himself."
—Josh Billings

Many clinics will allow owners to be present during euthanasia and there are even some veterinarians who will euthanize pets at their homes. Pet owners should determine what would be the least traumatic for their pets, and act accordingly. If the veterinarian is unable or unwilling to accommodate your preferences, request a referral.

Some people feel they could not be present during the process without becoming highly emotional and even incapacitated. Animals understand human emotions, to be sure, and any individual whose behavior could be traumatic to their pet should probably not be present during the process. But others feel their relationship with their pet compels them to be present so they can provide comfort in a final act of supreme love and bonding. They want to feel a sense of closure and take comfort in seeing their pet finally at peace. In such cases, the pet will likely feel more comfortable and secure and those owners would do well to stay, no matter how difficult it will be for them. Whether you choose to be present or not, it's a good idea to have a family member or close friend with you. They can offer you comfort and strength, and can even help you get home after all is done.

A pet owner will never do anything more difficult than witnessing the euthanasia of his or her pet, and it's understandable that many simply cannot do it. Those who choose not to be present should make sure their pets are going to be euthanized immediately, while they wait in the waiting room, or in the car. This is because some clinics wait until after working hours to perform the procedure. That prolongs the animal's suffering needlessly and will, in turn, add to the trauma it is experiencing.

And when the deed is done.

"The greatest love is a mother's; then a dog's;
then a sweetheart's."
—Polish Proverb

Your pet's final resting place is a matter that should be decided well in advance. Most people will become a little disoriented and some will be overcome by grief when they lose a pet. This complicates the process of determining the final disposition and is the worst time to determine the best course of action. Pet owners should be proactive in deciding on the final disposition of their pets, especially if they want to make special arrangements for a funeral, memorial, or internment. You should determine ahead of time whether or not you will cremate the remains, bury them somewhere, or simply leave them with the veterinarian to dispose of at his discretion.

There are other complex issues to consider, such as those associated with spiritual beliefs. Some may embrace the beliefs discussed in the first section of this book, while others may consider death the final chapter of a pet's existence. Some may want to keep their pet's remains close to them, possibly in an urn kept in the home, or in a location that had significance for the pet (i.e. buried in the back yard near its favorite tree). Others may not care what happens to the remains because they consider them nothing more than "dust" and devoid of their pet's true essence. Whatever the case, pet owners who take care to do what they believe is right for the pet are likely to find closure and healing quicker than those who leave the decisions to someone else.

You can choose a number of different options for the final disposition of your pet's remains. For example, you can choose home burial, a practice that is typically permitted in rural and suburban settings. This affords you the benefit of planning a funeral or memorial service at minimal expense. It also gives you the opportunity to landscape or design the setting of the internment. A non-biodegradable or self-vaulting container will help safeguard your pet's remains. This option it not without problems, however. For instance, some municipal codes prohibit pet burials on private property. Home burial is also a bad option for renters or homeowners who know they will not be staying at that location.

Sentiment is another problem related to burial. Many owners like to landscape a pet's final resting place with flowering trees, statuary or benches. This facilitates closure and, for some people, encourages visitations to the site. When owners choose to inter their pets on their own land, they must be aware that the location could become a constant reminder of their sorrow, and they may find themselves avoiding the area in order to be spared ongoing emotional pain that should have been left behind. Also, those who plant a special tree, flower or bush at the site could be traumatized if it dies prematurely.

Many pet owners choose a pet cemetery as the final resting place of their pet. Such locations provide a sense of dignity, security, and permanence. Owners find comfort in knowing their pets are resting permanently in a place that is peaceful and serene. Pet cemeteries are becoming increasingly popular and can be found in many populated areas. Most have made arrangements to ensure the land will not be converted to other uses in the future and make provisions for grooming and maintenance well into the future. But cost may be a deterrent to choosing this option and some owners may resort to communal burial. Burying your pet with others should in no way be considered "undignified" or less than what the animal deserves.

Cremation is the option of choice for many pet owners. It is less expensive and it presents a number of different options for the final disposition. Once a pet is cremated, the remains can be kept in a decorative urn or placed in a pet mausoleum. They can be scattered in a preferred location or simply buried in the owner's backyard (which is legal in most locations). In some areas, communal cremation is a sensible alternative. Many pet cemeteries have their own crematoriums and pets are often cremated along with other pets. Like communal burial, your pet's dignity is in no way affected by cremation with other animals.

Having to explain it all to the children

"I think dogs are the most amazing creatures; they give unconditional love. For me they are the role model for being alive."
—Gilda Radner

A common mistake pet owners make is assuming their children are too young to understand when a pet dies. They are, of course, the best judges of what their children should know and how they should be told. In most instances, it's best to be honest and forthright about the loss, and to encourage children to express their beliefs, fears, and concerns. We should never criticize or mock a child when he cries or tell her she should be strong and not feel sad. Anything you say about the animal's status after death should be sincere and based upon personal beliefs and convictions. It is unwise to make promises you can't explain or justify, and you may do your pet a disservice if you tell your child something that is no more credible than the Tooth Fairy, Easter Bunny, or Santa Claus.

Children tend to emulate their parents and when they see one trying to hide or cover up their sorrow and grief, they may do likewise. This could do harm to both parent and child. Every member of the family is unique, and each should be allowed to sort through his feelings and emotions as he sees fit and at his own pace.

Finally, pet owners must be honest with their children. When parents fabricate stories to protect the children, they often end up hurting them. Some children do not understand when they're told their pet "went to sleep," and may think it's only a matter of time before it wakes up. Telling a child that a pet "went away" is also discouraged. Some children will blame themselves and wonder what they did to cause the pet to leave. Others may expect it to return at any time and struggle as the days pass and the pet simply doesn't come home. Children who watch and wait, expecting the imminent return of their pet, may experience difficulty in accepting a new pet and may require special attention.

CHAPTER NINE

PICKING UP THE PIECES OF A BROKEN HEART

And in the aftermath, grief!

"Recollect that the Almighty, who gave the dog to be companion of our pleasures and our toils, hath invested him with a nature noble and incapable of deceit."
—Sir Walter Scott

Grief is the deep mental anguish a person experiences as a result of losing a loved one, including a pet. Not surprisingly, it is a well-documented fact that animals can also go through a grieving process when they lose a human "master" or companion animal. Grief is a necessary part of our character, because it heightens our appreciation of the beauty of love as well as the sanctity of life. The capacity to love is one of the greatest gifts God gave to His creation and grief is the only other feeling people experience that can match love in intensity and depth. Grief is profound and complicated. No other feeling or emotion hurts us as much as grief which reaches down into the very roots of a person's soul. Though universal, the effects of grief are unique to the individual and depend on a number of different circumstances.

The grief a person experiences from the loss of a pet depends on a number of factors. The nature or closeness of the relationship, and the uncertainty of not knowing whether or not a person will see his or her pet again are among the many factors that can contribute to grief. When we lose a family member, a friend, or a beloved animal, we are reminded of our mortality and the inevitability of our own demise. We're also reminded that we do not have the power to control our destinies as some would believe. Such a realization can be difficult to cope with and only adds to the despair a person feels with the loss of a loved one.

Those of us who have been close to a pet have enjoyed the unconditional love that only an animal can give. This is not an automatic love, but one that is acquired over time, and one that is based upon shared experiences. The responsibility of nurturing and caring for a pet fulfills an innate need that humans have and it strengthens the bonding process. Ironically, while these things draw us closer to our animals, they also add to the grief we experience when we lose them.

Not all grief is the same

"It's funny how dogs and cats know the inside of
folks better than other folks do, isn't it?"
—Eleanor H. Porter "Pollyanna" 1912

Because of the way society as a whole perceives pets, e.g. "after all, they're only animals", we tend to grieve their loss differently than we do for people. Many people poke fun at those who openly grieve the loss of a pet and cannot understand why people would wonder whether or not animals go to heaven. Our beliefs can sometimes cause confusion and division within the church and even among friends and family members. Because of these and other reasons, many people prefer to deal privately with the loss of a pet.

Guilt can result for a number of different reasons, and is another factor that can contribute to our grief. For example, some pet owners who felt compelled to end the suffering of a pet by euthanasia, find themselves struggling with their decision long after the deed is done. And while it was undoubtedly the best, if not the only, decision they could have made, they cannot help but feel as though they've convicted and executed a dear companion without so much as a trial. Others, who took too much time, or chose not to make the decision at all, may eventually realize they prolonged their pet's suffering unnecessarily.

Other factors, such as the belief that they didn't do enough for their pet, can contribute to guilt-based grief. How many of us take time off from work when a pet dies or seek closure by means of a formal ceremony such as a funeral? And, how many of us choose to have our pets cremated, only to leave the disposition of their ashes to someone else? But doing too much can also lead to guilt. For example, those who seek closure by means of a formal, elaborate ritual can experience guilt when they begin to realize they may have gone too far.

For the Christian, the feelings associated with the loss of a pet can differ from those associated with the loss of a human. Biblical and church teachings are clear with respect to humans and the afterlife. But, many pet owners don't know how to search scripture for answers to their questions about animals and eternity. They consequently tend to stretch or embellish their beliefs to make them fit their own situations. Others may think turning to *The Bible* for answers is simply inappropriate. These and other factors can lead to confusion, division, or frustration, and those feelings can lead to guilt.

Grief is a process

"If a dog jumps in your lap, it is because he is fond of you; but if a cat does the same thing, it is because your lap is warmer."
—Alfred North Whitehead

Problem recognition must always precede problem solving. While individuals vary, most of us can expect to progress through a number of predictable stages as we navigate the grieving process. Once we realize where we are in the journey, we can better understand the process and learn to cope with our loss.

Denial is usually the first stage of the grief process. This is a natural reaction to our loss where our minds work overtime in order to soften the initial trauma. Denial can manifest itself as disbelief, or it may even take the form of subtle hallucinations. Some people believe they see or hear their pet at certain times, as if it were still with them. In fact, people sometimes experience the presence of a pet days, weeks, or months after death has occurred. This phenomenon can be frightening or disorienting to some people, but others may actually find it comforting. Many professionals who do bereavement counseling believe that hallucinatory experiences in grief are actually an important, if not vital, part of healing.

When we lose a precious companion, it can be very hard to accept the fact that it is really gone. Our brains accept the reality of death, but our "hearts" tell us otherwise. This clash of emotions can become the catalyst for internal strife. To make matters worse, anything in our surroundings can be a constant reminder of our cherished pets.

Denial can also manifest itself in strange emotional reactions. While most of us are moved to tears when a pet dies, some of us experience outbursts of anger, unusual laughter, or other odd behavior. Others feel as though they're existing in a surreal world, or even dreaming their current reality. We must expect the unexpected and be prepared to accommodate others as they struggle with accepting the reality of pet loss.

Bargaining is typically the next step in the grieving process. Christians may try to make deals with God so that their pet will be spared the inevitable. Others resolve to themselves and promise to do things differently if their companion survives. This stage is sometimes predicated on guilt, and some people may feel their own conduct may have somehow contributed to the death of their pet. They swear to themselves, or to God, that they now recognize the error of their ways and vow to never repeat their mistakes. These individuals are willing to promise anything—whatever it takes to hang on to their beloved pets.

Anger and/or Guilt normally comes next. Depending on the person and the circumstances, anger can manifest itself in a number of ways. Some individuals internalize their anger over the loss of a pet, which only leads to other problems. Others express their anger outwardly, acting aggressively toward others. This reaction to loss may help an individual in the short-term by providing momentary relief, but it can also have an adverse impact on relationships over the long-term. Remember, doubts, confusion, and ambivalence are all natural responses to the trauma of losing a pet, and we shouldn't be surprised when we find ourselves feeling overwhelmed by them.

When anger is internalized, it can turn into guilt which may be directed inward, e.g. "if only I hadn't...". Anger may also manifest itself outwardly, e.g. "You said you could help my pet, but now he's dead! It's your fault!" There are steps grieving pet owners can take that may lead to relief from anger and guilt. For example, they should acknowledge they have absolutely no control over the past. Telling themselves they "could have..." or "should have..." is senseless and harmful. When they find themselves fretting over such concerns, they should recognize it for the harmful behavior it is and command themselves to "STOP!" One way to neutralize this problem is to write down the guilt-related things they're telling themselves and then, pledge to themselves they will never mention or think about them again. Some may want to post a list in a conspicuous location and read it every day until the feelings of guilt disappear. Others might prefer to throw the list away, in a symbolic gesture of ridding themselves of the guilt.

When there is an element of truth in the guilt a person is feeling, they should remember what God tells us about forgiveness. They should ask what it would take to forgive themselves, and then do it. They can even say, "I forgive you" as many times as it takes.

Sometimes it is helpful to try a little role-playing where grieving people pretend to be their own best friend. Pet owners who feel guilt can then ask themselves what they could say to dispel those feelings. They can even put themselves in their pet's place and try to imagine what their pet would say about the guilt they have imposed upon themselves. Participation in a pet grief support group is another good way to beat the feeling of guilt because grieving pet owners can obtain forgiveness and absolution from others.

Another effective way people can minimize guilt is to focus on the sacrifices and all the good things they did for their pets. Individuals who are struggling with pet loss should dwell on the many ways they expressed their love for their companions by giving them the care and nurture they needed. They may find it helpful to write those things down and read them whenever they feel the onset of guilt. They can also try to refocus their guilt into something that can be helpful to others. If they've learned valuable lessons from their experience, they can share them with other pet owners, possibly sparing them and their animals of having to endure unnecessary hardships.

Grief usually displaces anger. Once a person finally comes to terms with the fact that his or her pet is really gone, the grieving process begins. Some will arrive at this stage fairly quickly, while others may suffer for weeks, months or longer before grasping the reality of their loss. But beware, getting beyond anger and guilt sometimes accentuates the emptiness a person feels. While most of us are "wired" to cope with this emptiness, some may need to seek professional help. If allowed to continue for long periods, this aspect of the grieving process can lead to apathy, withdrawal or the inability to cope with reality. Veterinarians, trained grief counselors and professionals who work for pet cemeteries are all possible sources of support for people struggling to deal with the grief.

Those who lose a pet must realize that they're not the first or only ones to experience such pain and that it is perfectly normal to express their grief. Sadly, many of us feel too embarrassed to do so even though our pain is very real and not just imagined. The Bible does not command Christians to keep a "stiff upper lip" while negotiating the valley of grief. The pain associated with the loss of a beloved pet is not diminished in any way just because we're Christians. Our reputations and our testimonies are not dependent upon whether or not we display emotion while coping with a broken heart. Neither God nor man benefits when we deny our pain or refuse to cry after losing a pet. A griever should be allowed to cry because crying is a natural and normal coping mechanism. Some researchers have found that crying out of sadness triggers hormonal changes that are therapeutic. As most women already know, it's okay to cry.

Christians are blessed in many ways, but immunity to pain and suffering is not promised anywhere in God's word. We should demonstrate our integrity by honestly facing the harsh realities of our earthly journey. As we struggle to overcome our grief, we must not allow ourselves to feel we're betraying our pets by trying to overcome our loss. Grief is simply a part of the healing process and, while it should not be carried to the extreme, it should be allowed to run its course. In dealing with grief, we can never lose sight of the comforting words Paul wrote to the Roman church:

And we know that all things work together for good to them that love God, to them who are called according to his purpose. Romans 8:28 (KJV)

Acceptance is normally the final stage of the grieving process. Time is the master healer that eventually allows pleasant memories to replace the grief and sadness. Most of us will come to terms with the loss of a beloved companion and make the necessary adjustments to life without our pets within a 6-month period. While in Vietnam, I once told a military chaplain that I knew I was going to have a lot of bad memories of my experience there. He replied, "No, you'll have good memories about bad times." He was absolutely right. As we work our way through the grieving process, we find ourselves focusing on pleasant memories and will even want to share them with others. As the chaplain predicted, we'll even have precious memories about the bad times we shared with our pets.

Once we finally arrive at this plateau, we'll know we've completed the grieving process. Acceptance means making decisions and moving on. Life will be different, but it is not over. And while it may be different, it will still be good, because of the goodness of the God we serve:

O give thanks unto the Lord; for he is good: because his mercy endureth for ever. Ps 118:1(KJV)

I called upon the Lord in distress: the Lord answered me, and set me in a large place. The Lord is on my side; I will not fear: what can man do unto me? The Lord taketh my part with them that help me: therefore shall I see my desire upon them that hate me. It is better to trust in the Lord than to put confidence in man. Ps 118:5-8 (KJV)

Acceptance, the final stage of grief, is where mourners come to regard their loss as a growth-promoting experience that has helped them to become better Christians. It changes their entire outlook on life and affords them a deeper awareness of its fragility as well as a richer appreciation for its beauty and importance.

No one enjoys the pain of loss. But those who choose not to have another pet because they are afraid of facing the eventuality of another loss, are only depriving themselves of another priceless relationship. Faith in the one who will never abandon us will enable us to risk loving again. It is absolutely essential that we learn to trust in God's enduring love as the only thing that will sustain us in the difficult process of grief. The desire to have and love another pet is the best indicator that all stages of grief have been successfully completed.

Can anything good come from grief?

"If a cat does something, we call it instinct; if we do the same thing, for the same reason, we call it intelligence."
—Will Cuppy

Character is forged in the fires of loss and grief. God calls on us to use even the painful circumstances of our lives to deepen our reliance on Him. It is in the context of darkness that painful losses generate a revealing light showing us God's goodness. By understanding where we will be going, we will be better prepared to handle the loss when it comes. Though painful, we must face the loss of a pet head-on in order to truly come to terms with it. This brings us to a starting point where we can begin to rebuild our shattered world.

As Christians, we know God created us with the capacity to grieve, an important part of our psychological make-up. Still, we can't help but wonder why God would burden us with such a painful trait. But, as is always the case, we only have to turn to God's word to find the answer to this question:

> *We rejoice in the hope of the glory of God. Not only so, but we also rejoice in our sufferings, because we know that suffering produces perseverance; perseverance, character; and character, hope. And hope does not disappoint us, because God has poured out His love into our hearts by the Holy Spirit, whom He has given us. Romans 5:25 (NIV)*

Paul says we should "rejoice in our suffering," not because God wants for us to dwell in pain, but because our suffering produces perseverance, character, and hope. Facing a loss, whether it is a death or some other traumatic life event, leads us to Christian maturity. Grief provides the opportunity for a person to discover their own true character, as well as what's really important in life. No one is ever the same after experiencing a significant loss. As difficult as it may be, it is not beyond our ability to endure. On a hill in Galilee, Jesus promised us:

> *Blessed are those who mourn, for they shall be comforted. Matthew 5:4 (KJV)*

Paul, who wrote much of the New Testament, assured us nothing in this life can separate us from God's unfailing love:

> *For I am persuaded, that neither death, nor life, nor angels, nor principalities, nor powers, nor things present, nor things to come, Nor height, nor depth, nor any other creature, shall be able to separate us from the love of God, which is in Christ Jesus our Lord. Romans 8:38-39*

When we feel we have lost everything, we can take comfort in knowing we still have God's love. We know God is our ever-present companion, and is there at our side as we make our way through life's painful experiences. The rod and staff of Psalm 23:4 symbolizes the Lord's loving presence and the protection we need to negotiate the treacherous journey of life.

Realistically, we know the pain of loss will never disappear completely, and reminiscing will always bring some discomfort and even tears. But, along with that pain comes a heightened appreciation for

God's creation, a blessing that comes only after a journey through the life-changing valley of grief. Simply put, grief over any loss can have a healthy effect if it brings us closer to God. Our sense of tragedy can be good for us if it puts us among the multitudes who have sought comfort, deliverance, and blessings at the foot of the cross.

CHAPTER TEN

GONE, BUT NOT FORGOTTEN

When it's time to move on

"I like pigs. Dogs look up to us. Cats look down on us.
Pigs treat us as equals."
—Winston Churchill

The loss of a pet is a personal experience to be sure, but it doesn't have to be faced alone. There are a number of different ways we can obtain help with coping. Those who are struggling to deal with such a loss can obtain interactive help from the local church, online Internet bereavement groups, pet-loss support hotlines and pet bereavement counseling services. *The Bible*, books, videos, and magazine articles can also be helpful in learning to cope with the loss.

Before we can seek help, we must first acknowledge our grief and then, allow ourselves to express it. We can do this in a number of ways. We can reach out to others who might lend a sympathetic ear. A call to a veterinarian, an animal shelter, or the local humane society may help locate a pet loss support group. Another good way to express our grief is to simply write about it in a journal or perhaps a poem. If you don't feel up to talking to someone or writing about your loss, you can simply turn it over to God in prayer.

As pet owners make their way through the grieving process, they should watch for changes in themselves that may indicate the onset of depression, a serious medical problem. For example:

✓ You find yourself losing interest in things that used to be important to you;
✓ You are not eating regularly, or are less interested in your appearance and personal hygiene;

✓ Your normal sleep pattern has changed, sleeping too little or too much;

✓ You find yourself withdrawing and choosing to ignore friends or not leave the house.

People who find themselves experiencing any of these changes should consider seeking professional help. Sometimes the simple act of talking with others is enough to jump-start the healing process.

Returning to work, attending social events or starting a hobby can all be good ways to get back on track. It also helps to get back into the swing of daily routine such as a job or taking care of the needs of your household. Diversion therapy is another effective tool that can help mourners return to normalcy after the loss of a pet. Simple projects and gestures that occupy our hearts and our hands are often more than enough to provide the necessary motivation to move onward. Here are a few examples:

✓ Plant a tree or a shrub and dedicate it to your beloved companion with a small plaque;

✓ Dedicate a spot somewhere on your property and designate it as a memorial to your pet;

✓ Purchase a book and place a label inside the front cover inscribed, "In memory of (your pet's name). Then donate the book to a school or library;

✓ Share anecdotes and favorite stories about the pet with others. Let people know it's your way of keeping the memories alive;

✓ Create a multi-seasonal wreath with pictures, toys, and items that belonged to your pet for display in your home or at the animal's grave site;

✓ Make a donation to a favorite charity in honor of your pet;

✓ Wrap framed pictures of your pet and present them as a gifts to other grieving family members;

✓ Include your pet's name in family prayers, especially during meals;

✓ Create a special Christmas ornament or decoration with the name or photo of your pet;

✓ Decorate a candle and light it during family times in memory of your pet;

✓ Encourage grieving children to draw pictures and create gifts inspired by their memories of their pet;

✓   Create a decoration that represents your hopes and dreams for
the future and hang it in a prominent place.

It's not enough to keep your hands busy. You must keep your mind
busy as well. If you feel you're thinking about your pet constantly and
can't seem to stop, then make your thoughts happy ones. For example,
dwell on thoughts such as these:

✓   How did I get my pet?
✓   How did I feel the first time I saw my pet?
✓   How did my pet get its name?
✓   What was special about my pet?
✓   What did we do to have fun?
✓   What are the special moments we enjoyed together?

Helping others get through the process

*"In order to keep a true perspective of one's importance,
everyone should have a dog that will worship him and a cat
that will ignore him."*
—Dereke Bruce

Those of us who have experienced the loss of a pet have a lot to offer
others when they suffer such a loss. But helping someone else cope
with grief can be a delicate process and we must be extremely careful.

Remember, every situation is unique. It doesn't matter what kind of
animal a person is grieving. He or she may have been as fond of a pet
lizard or a tarantula as you are of a puppy or kitten. All that matters is
that these individuals are hurting. Remember, the uniqueness of our per-
sonalities means we all handle circumstances differently. When people
are grieving, you can be most helpful by being sincere, non-judgmental,
and truly concerned about their feelings. It doesn't matter if a person
experiences something differently than you did. This is their grief, and
they need to find ways to deal with it on their own terms.

It can help if you acknowledge a person's loss in a tangible way such
as a telephone call or even an email. Don't tell them you know how they
feel (you may not), but tell them you're sorry and understand that it is
extremely difficult for them. Don't make cryptic references to the pet's

name (i.e. "little one," "your companion," "your cat," etc). Use the animal's actual name in your comments, because it personalizes your words and makes them more than "generic."

If you have the time and ability, offer to be with them. This may be especially helpful if this person has to take the pet to the vet, especially if euthanasia is a possible outcome. If that isn't possible, at least let them know you're "there for them" via telephone. Let them know you're praying for them, and consider inviting them to pray with you.

Some people, especially men, may not want to talk during times of grief. If they want you to be there, but don't want to talk or be talked to, let them know you understand and then, respect their wishes. Sometimes your presence is enough and you should be prepared to comfort them in silence. If someone needs to talk in order to get things off his or her chest, let them do so. Don't try to comment on everything they say. You can sometimes speak volumes by saying nothing at all. Encourage them to be honest with you and to let you know what they prefer.

The spoken word is fleeting, but thoughts expressed in writing can be permanent. A personal visitation or a phone call can do wonders for those who grieve. But people can be comforted over and over again by a simple note or letter consisting of a poem, personal remembrance of the pet, or an expression of sorrow and concern.

Be sincere. In our modern society, we often do things out of a sense of obligation or try to say things we don't actually feel, because we want to say what we think others want to hear. Any appearance of insincerity could hurt your friend or family member deeply. If you really don't know what to say, then tell them so. If you wish you could take their pain away, tell them that too. And remember, your help and support does not end after your initial expression of support. Follow through and stay in touch on a regular basis. Over the course of time, you'll learn to know when this person is ready to move on.

Consider offering help with the person's daily routine. If they are distraught, they may not be able to function and perform certain tasks around the house or on the job. On the other hand, people sometimes need to be occupied so they won't dwell on their circumstances.

A nice hug, or a simple pat on the arm or shoulder can do wonders for some people. But such gestures can also be highly offensive to others, even those you think you know. The safest bet is to simply ask someone if they would like a hug.

Men's emotions are as deep and profound as women's, but many men struggle when they try to express their feelings. If it appears a person who is grieving the loss of a pet is about to cry or be overcome by emotion, simply tell them, "It's OK." Internalizing our emotions is self-destructive, and we should do all we can to facilitate the outward expression of feelings without dragging them out of someone. Sometimes, it's possible to get someone to begin the process by simply asking the right questions, such as: "Do you feel like talking about it?" or "How are you coping?" Sometimes you can ask them to tell you how they acquired the pet or how they picked the animal's name. You can even share some personal experiences you had with the pet.

When someone indicates they're feeling guilty, don't try to justify their past actions or try to relieve them of their guilt. Encourage them to tell you how they were feeling at the time they acted the way they did and to discuss what else was going on. A person who loses a job may not have the income to pay for expensive medical treatments. And someone who has commitments may not be able to spend a lot of time with their pets. Try not to draw or form opinions, and encourage the grieving person to explore the issues associated with their actions themselves.

Be careful when giving your friend a book or video/audio tape. You should know what beliefs and recommendations are represented, and whether or not the grieving person shares those beliefs. No matter how well intended, a gift representing certain religious beliefs or other topics related to animals could be offensive to some individuals. If you do give such a gift, don't ask him or her if they enjoyed it, because you may put them in an awkward position.

If you're not careful...

*"Don't accept your dog's admiration as conclusive
evidence that you are wonderful."*
—Ann Landers

Words can have a profound effect on someone who is grieving the loss of a pet, and you must choose them wisely. You should be especially careful to avoid the use of clichés. Many people consider them insincere and even offensive, especially if they promote a belief the grieving person does not share. The following are examples of clichés some people may not care to hear and you should avoid using then when trying to comfort someone who has lost a pet:

✓   "You're sure taking it well;"
✓   "Don't worry, you'll get over it;"
✓   "You should be grateful he lived such a long life;"
✓   "I know just how you feel;"
✓   "You can just be thankful that at least you still have [name of other pet(s)];"
✓   "It was just a dog; you can always get another one;"
✓   "Don't cry, this will all pass;"
✓   "There's a reason for everything, and it was just your pet's time to die;"
✓   "It was God's will, so just accept it and move on."

Don't overwhelm a grieving person by telling him or her how wonderful your current pet is or how well you managed to overcome the loss of a pet sometime in your past. Remember, this is not about you, and such remarks may cause resentment. If the grieving person indicates an interest in talking about such things, then follow their lead. Otherwise, give them plenty of breathing room so they can make sense out of what has happened to their world.

Don't try to mitigate the loss by comparing the grieving person's loss to your own or anyone else's. Don't tell him or her that, "it could have been much worse." The facts associated with someone else's loss of a pet are not important. All that matters is that this person is struggling. Don't remind him or her that, "at least their pet didn't suffer like so-and-so's," or "unlike so-and-so, at least they know what happened to their pet."

A grieving person may seem incoherent or disorganized when trying to express his or her feelings. He or she might exhibit mood swings, anger or irrational behavior. Someone mourning a loss may break from their normal routine by letting the grass grow or the dirty dishes pile up. This is normal to a point and can be expected. Be careful not to criticize them or push them to act any differently, unless enough time has passed for them to have completed their grieving process. When a grieving person attempts to express himself, don't interrupt or try to put words in his or her mouth. And most importantly, don't scold him or give the appearance of being impatient (e.g. "Come on, get over it!"). Sometimes it's best to simply be a passive listener.

Grieving people will eventually reach the point where they are ready to get on with rest of their lives and put their loss behind them. Here's where it can get a little tricky. Some individuals will not want to discuss their loss any more and prefer to look ahead to the future.

Others, however, will want to talk about their pets and will welcome any opportunity to share pleasant thoughts and memories. Don't try to convince your friend that "enough is enough," and that "it's time to move on." They are the only ones who can make that determination. If you exercise patience and are observant, what's best for this person will become evident soon enough.

Give grieving persons all the room they need, and don't try to engage them in any situations or problems that you're dealing with in your own life. Your role should be that of giving, not receiving. You may need to leave them alone as they find their way, and may have to be careful about just "dropping in," depending on their personal needs. This doesn't mean you have to cross to the other side of the street when you see them coming, or let the answer machine screen all your phone calls. If you're uncomfortable, or don't know how to act around a grieving friend, be sincere and let him or her know you're not sure what to do. But assure them that you truly want to support them in any way you can. Your support could have a profound and lasting impact on your future relationship with that person.

CHAPTER ELEVEN

THE LAST WORD

When should I replace my pet?

*"Women and cats will do as they please, and men and
dogs should relax and get used to the idea."*
—*Robert A. Heinlein*

Many people feel compelled to rush out and get another pet as soon
as possible. They sometimes do so because family and friends encourage them to replace the pet right away. Some people even acquire a
"replacement" before their pet dies, believing it will soften the loss.
Others take their time replacing their pet so they can sort through their
feelings and settle into a coping strategy. It's a sad reality that many
people never replace their companions at all because they don't want
to experience the pain of another loss ever again.

Is there a right answer? No; it depends on a number of factors.
People need time to grieve and heal, and should take all the time they
need to attend to the profound feelings they experience when dealing
with the loss of a pet. A new pet will require a lot of time and attention,
and many people are not ready to devote time and attention to a new
pet until they've successfully completed the grieving process.

When people replace their pets prematurely, they run the risk of
feeling resentment towards the new pet because it is seen as trying to
"take the place" of the old pet. Some people, especially children, may
feel that they're being "disloyal" to the previous pet. Another reason to
wait is the message that premature replacement can send to your children. It tends to take away from the love and memories they have for
the deceased animal and makes them think something of value can be
easily replaced.

We should acquire a new pet after we have put the past behind us and are ready to move forward in a brand new relationship. When we think the time has come to get a new pet, we should make it a family decision and involve the children in the discussion, as well as in the selection. Everyone needs to play a role in the process, and participating in the selection strengthens the bonding process early on.

When selecting a new pet, it's wise to avoid getting a "look-alike" animal. We should also give it a different name and nickname. Otherwise, we'll find ourselves making unfair comparisons, and the new pet will be subjected to unrealistic expectations. We must let the pet develop its own personality and relationships with all the people in its new world.

A word about pets grieving pets

"If you want a kitten, start out by asking for a horse."
—Naomi, 15 (Advice from Kids)

As many pet owners know, animals can go through a grieving process similar to our own when they lose a person or companion pet. Some animals know something is wrong when a companion exhibits signs of illness or old age, or is absent for more than a day. When animals grieve, they typically show signs of sadness or depression. They may frequently search the house or backyard, lose interest in eating, or act out of character. Unfortunately, there is not much that can be done in such cases, and it's best to consult your veterinarian for advice.

In closing

"The dog has seldom been successful in pulling man
up to its level of sagacity, but man has frequently
dragged a dog down to his."
—James Thurber

No matter how well prepared you think you are, you should expect to suffer when you lose a pet. This is normal and, in some ways, healthy. Most of us simply cannot comprehend what life will be like without our pets. It seems everything we see, hear, smell, or touch reminds us of our little companions. Many of us choose to surround ourselves with keepsakes and mementos, which is normal and healthy to a point. But, we must guard against becoming obsessive or unwilling to put the past behind and move ahead. At some point, we have to move from mourning the loss of our pet to celebrating the relationship we enjoyed.

What we choose to hang on to, and how long we hang on to it, is our choice. There is nothing wrong with honoring the memory of our pets by cherishing their favorite toys, photographs of them, or other keepsakes that remind us of what they were. But we cannot lose sight of the fact that we are all subject to God's design for the cycle of life.

Jesus once said we should "let the dead bury the dead." He wanted us to know that life must go on for the living and that we should not deny ourselves the future blessings He has to offer us by dwelling on a past over which we have no control. *The Bible* tells us that God wants us to express our needs to Him, then surrender our will in faith, knowing that He will take care of us.

> *Be anxious for nothing, but in everything by prayer and supplication, with thanksgiving, let your requests be made known to God; Philippians 4:6 (NKJV™)*

> *Casting all your care upon Him, for He cares for you. 1 Peter 5:7 (NKJV™)*

REFERENCES

0-595-32228-X

Made in the USA
Columbia, SC
20 August 2017